Walt Disney

TREASURES

THE OFFICIAL ANNIVERSARY BOOK

Stephen A. Geppi, *President/Publisher and Chief Executive Officer;* John K. Snyder Jr., *Chief Administrative Officer.* STAFF: Leonard (John) Clark, *Editor-in-Chief;* Sue Kolberg, *Assistant Editor;* Travis Seitler, *Art Director;* David Gerstein, *Archival Editor;* Melissa Bowersox, *Director-Creative Projects.* CONTRIBUTING STAFF: Gary Leach, Susan Daigle-Leach, *Art & Editorial.* ADVERTISING/MARKETING: J.C. Vaughn, *Executive Editor;* Brenda Busick, *Creative Director;* Jamie David, *Director of Marketing;* Sara Ortt, *Marketing Assistant, ads@gemstonepub.com;* Heather Winter, *Office Manager, Toll Free (888) 375-9800 Ext. 249;* Mark Huesman, *Production Assistant;* Mike Wilbur, *Shipping Manager;* Ralph Turner, *Accounting Manager;* Angie Meyer, Judy Goodwin, *Subscriptions, Toll Free (800) 322-7978.*

Walt Disney Treasures
Disney Comics: 75 Years of Innovation

75 YEARS OF INNOVATION

by David Gerstein

Walt Disney often said that his cartoon empire "all started with a Mouse." But Disney animation existed before Mickey. It can also be argued that without the novelty of sound, the famed rodent would never have been an empire-starter. Now, to say that Disney's comic book empire started with a Mouse? That's more like it—there were no Disney comics before Mickey! Beginning with the Mouse and moving ahead, entire schools of creativity sprang up on multiple continents, hosting some of the medium's most creative innovators. So many greats have worked with Disney comics, in fact, that this—our official 75th anniversary book—can only begin to chronicle some of the exciting moments that our favorite mice, ducks, and dogs have experienced over the years.

Disney comics were born on January 13, 1930, with the launch of the Mickey Mouse daily newspaper strip. The strip's early gag stories, exemplified in this book by "Mickey Mouse Music" (1930), were soon supplanted by the adventure serials of Floyd Gottfredson, a master Mouse plotter with a unique take on Mickey's gang. The result, elaborate sagas like this book's "Foray to Mount Fishflake" (1934), were an international hit—and Mickey was an adventuresome, two-fisted international star. This led to the birth of a comic strip department within Disney—and the start of the *Silly Symphony* companion strip, in which artist Al Taliaferro refined the up-and-coming Donald Duck.

It also spawned a move into a new medium: Disney comic strips led to Disney comic books. In the 1930s, most such titles—exemplified by Western Publishing's *Mickey Mouse Magazine*—featured newspaper strip reprints. But some, like Britain's *Mickey Mouse Annual,* featured first-run comics production. Following the precedent set by the American newspaper strips, European Disney creators started out producing simple gag pages—like Wilfred Haughton's "Scoutmaster Mickey"—but quickly moved into longer-form sagas. By the end of the decade, English and Italian creators were writing and drawing the first long Donald Duck adventure stories.

The 1940s saw our domestic creators playing a masterful game of catch-up. As the "Golden Age" of American comics hit its stride, Western editor Eleanor Packer transformed *Mickey Mouse Magazine* into the 64-page *Walt Disney's Comics and Stories,* the first modern-style Disney comics title. Thicker than any previous periodical, *WDC&S* had room enough to reprint long Gottfredson Mickey epics one after another. But by 1942, Packer's newspaper strip backlog began to run low. If Western wanted more comics and stories, they would have to produce them themselves.

And so they did—putting the star power of Carl Barks, former Disney animation story man, behind Donald Duck. Like Gottfredson before him, "good Duck artist" Barks brought new subtleties to his funny animal hero; also like Gottfredson, Barks created an entire world of vibrant new supporting players. Two of the most famous, Gladstone Gander and Uncle Scrooge, are featured in this volume's "Race to the South Seas." Barks' creations proved that Disney comics stars could match the popularity of their on-screen relatives.

It was an emboldening realization for Western and for Disney's comic strip department, both of which hit their stride in the 1940s. Li'l Bad Wolf, Big Bad's goody-goody son, was created by editor Chase Craig, later meeting his definitive writer/artist in Gil Turner. Carl Buettner drew new tales of Bucky Bug, hero of Junkville town, while artist Paul Murry served up smart Brer Rabbit in memorable swampland sagas. And Pogo's Walt Kelly, drawing early *WDC&S* gags during World War II, told of crafty Gremlin Gus and his saboteur Widget pals.

Another kind of battle followed in the 1950s: the Cold War, in which Western society was marked by popular conservatism and a new contention that comics were for kids. But Disney comics survived these social changes. While never just for kids, Disney comics were always kid-*friendly.* And they could be conservative and progressive at once—by stocking a deceptively simple, traditionalist world with surprisingly three-dimensional, desire-driven characters.

At the time, these characters included farmer gal Grandma Duck, retooled from Taliaferro origins; the Beagle Boys, inimitable Carl Barks nogoodniks; Ellsworth, the cynical mynah bird; Chip 'n' Dale, the pesky chipmunks; and Pluto, whose stories were narrated by scripter Don Christensen in a delightfully tongue-in-cheek style. This book's "Chipmunk Monkeyshines" pairs dog, 'munks, Christensen, and Paul Murry, known in the 1950s for his Mickey Mouse tales.

Mickey himself endured a shake-up in the 1950s, when changes at Disney's comic strip department put an end to Gottfredson's adventure continuities. This was significant because these serials were still the mainstay of *Topolino,* Italy's powerhouse Disney weekly. Publisher Mondadori was forced to create its own replacement serials, bringing future comics legends Romano Scarpa and Giorgio Cavazzano to Mickey's world. As shown by this volume's Ellsworth tale, "AKA Cormorant Number Twelve," the new Italian creators preserved Gottfredson's take on the Mickey gang. But they also introduced great new characters—here, the no-good Trudy Van Tubb—and an increasingly modern and abstract artistic style.

The 1960s would see modernity bringing other changes to Disney comics. Over the first few years of the new decade, the American Disney magazines' circulation fell from 1,375,000 copies per issue to three hundred thousand. Disney publications director George Sherman blamed television and rival publishers, but another problem, quality slippage, might have also been to blame. Once aimed at all ages, Western Publishing's stories had begun to acquire the kids-only flavor of non-Disney humor comics.

Some creators made the best of this. The good side of childish storytelling, after all, is the creative whimsy you can mine by doing it right. In 1964, Western editor Chase Craig and writer Del Connell created Goofy's secret identity of Super Goof: arguably too silly to fit into the worlds of Barks and Gottfredson, but good satire still. The Disney studio, meanwhile, began producing its own comics for overseas use in 1962, and these too shared the new tone of wild whimsy. The "Studio program's" star characters included obsessive beatnik Fethry Duck and cynical tomcat Tabby; created by storyman Dick Kinney and featured here in "The Retriever," they remain leading lights of European Disney comics to this day.

Even as "Studio program" stories ran through the press, however, foreign creators were producing more and more Disney tales of their own. In Italy, an entire school of writers and artists followed Scarpa's and Cavazzano's lead. In Denmark, editor Knut Dokker arranged for Gutenberghus Publishing Service, today's Egmont Creative A/S, to begin producing its own Donald Duck material. In Brazil, publisher Abril carried on the tales of José Carioca, *Saludos Amigos'* (1943) dapper parrot star. And Dutch publisher Oberon, occasional producers of new material as early as 1954, now ramped up production significantly.

The 1970s saw a new element giving strength to these initiatives. Called "Donaldism," it was a burgeoning fandom for Disney comics' 1940s golden age, and it led professional fans to mimic Barks' and Gottfredson's early works. Dutch editor Daan Jippes and his colleagues—including Fred Milton and Thom Roep—created lovingly elaborate Donald comedies, such as this volume's "Sauce for the Duck." In Denmark, editors Lars Bergström and Stefan Printz-Påhlson encouraged the same trend among their own writers and artists—among them Marck Meul, Daniel Branca, and Victor Arriagada Rios (Vicar). Our "A Witch In Crime" exemplifies the works of the era.

Disney comics scholarship came to Italy and Brazil too in the 1970s. But these countries' comic creators were too busy riding their own inspirations to take in much outside influence. Brazil's Renato Canini carried José Carioca to new heights—and comedic lows—with a heavy dose of authentic Rio culture. And Italian creators were busy creating popular new characters. The superheroic Duck Avenger, created in 1969, hit his stride in the decade following, while the 1980s saw Bruno Sarda's creation of Arizona Dipp, Goofy's daredevil cousin.

The 1980s was also the decade when Donaldism came to America. Western's comic books had hit a low point; sold only in toy stores and featuring generally weak material, they sputtered out in 1984. But Disney fans with printing presses were active elsewhere. 1980 saw collectors Russ Cochran and Bruce Hamilton form the publishing house Another Rainbow. Initially the publishers of *The Fine Art of Walt Disney's Donald Duck* (1980), a Carl Barks oil painting collection, and the famous *Carl Barks Library,* Another Rainbow followed on these successes by taking over the American Disney comic book license from Western.

With Byron Erickson as Editor-In-Chief, the new "Gladstone" comics imprint brought back Barks and Gottfredson, as well as giving European greats their first-ever exposure in English. But Erickson also produced first-run material, introducing the now-classic works of Don Rosa and William Van Horn. Rosa—represented in this book by his early "His Fortune on the Rocks"—sent Scrooge on numerous intricate treasure quests. "Loosey-goosey" William Van Horn took a different tack, drawing shorter and more comedic tales. Some, like the Gary Leach-written "Flights of Fancy," featured Launchpad McQuack, pilot star of the then-current *DuckTales* TV series.

DuckTales marked big changes at Disney. Revitalized by the early days of its Eisner and Katzenberg regime, it moved to exploit its comics properties as never before. Part of this plan, enacted in 1990, involved revoking Gladstone's license and publishing its own books in-house—which, while an ultimately unsuccessful effort, led to many new North American talents getting involved with ducks and mice. When Disney's plans imploded, these creators largely enlisted with Denmark's Egmont Creative A/S. The "Americans in Copenhagen" eventually included Don Rosa, William and Noel Van Horn, Janet and Michael T. Gilbert, Pat and Carol McGreal, John Lustig, Dave Rawson, and your present author, plus editors Byron Erickson (of Gladstone) and Bob Foster (of Disney).

This is not to say that Egmont, or any European publisher, has wanted for local creative talent in the 1990s or since. At Egmont, Lars Bergström, Stefan and Unn Printz-Påhlson, Henning Kure and other editors continue to produce "all-European" stories—including the notable work of writers Lars Jensen, Kari Korhonen, Gorm Transgaard, and Andreas Pihl. Modern-day Dutch stories—including the work of Jippes, writers Ruud Straatman and Frank Jonker, and artists Sander Gulien, Mau and Bas Heymans—have become internationally renowned. In Italy, finally, hyper-modern versions of Mickey, Duck Avenger, and the superheroic girls of *W. I. T. C. H.* have all enjoyed great success... though such non-traditional stories, great as they may be, lurk beyond the scope of this volume.

Here's to seventy-five years of Disney comics: seventy-five years of innovation, inspiration, and unforgettable creators. Legends like Carl Barks and Floyd Gottfredson have now passed on, but their heirs succeed the same way they succeeded—through simple respect for their readers and for their art form. Our comic stars may be talking animals, but our best works are not dumbed down; enslaved neither to the canard that kids require simplistic entertainment, nor to the superstition that older readers desire only easy self-parody. Artistic exploration and improvement have made the Disney magic for generations—and long may they continue to do so.

— David Gerstein

INTRODUCING—
THE WORLD FAMOUS MOVIE CHARACTER
MICKEY MOUSE
?
YM 004 (KFS 12/30/30-1/3/31)
WALT DISNEY
I'VE ALWAYS WANTED TO BE A MUSICIAN, MR. BUTT— COULD YOU SUGGEST A GOOD INSTRUMENT FOR ME TO PLAY? SOMETHING BIG AND IMPORTANT-LOOKING — LIKE THAT —
AW, SAY! YOU COULD NEVER BLOW THAT BIG-HORN — JUST A MINUTE—I HAVE THE VERY THING FOR YOU—
ALL KINDS OF MUSICAL INSTRUMENTS
WHAT— A PICCOLO? SA-AY, ARE YOU TRYING TO KID ME?
CERTAINLY NOT! THIS IS A FINE INSTRUMENT AND YOU COULD LEARN TO PLAY IT IN NO TIME—
ALL KINDS OF MUSICAL INSTRUMENTS
WELL, IT LOOKS AWFULLY PUNY— BUT GUESS IT'S MY SPEED- F IT JUST DIDN'T LOOK SO SISSIFIED—
OH, I CAN TAKE CARE OF THAT— I'VE GOT A SWELL CARRYING CASE I CAN LET YOU HAVE FOR IT—
THAT GUY'S NOT SO DUMB—
WILL BUTT, MUSICAL INSTRUMENTS
HOW TO PLAY THE PICCOLO

HEY! CAN YOU PLAY IT?
YOU BET I CAN — I'M AN EXPERT!
WELL, HOW ABOUT PLAYING ME A TUNE?
WHAT'S THIS- RAIN?
AW, SHUX!
STICK AROUND, KID—WE WON'T LET A LITTLE THING LIKE RAIN GET US DOWN—
I'LL BET MINNIE WILL BE SURPRISED WHEN SHE HEARS THIS SONG I'VE WRITTEN — LET'S SEE NOW, JUST A FEW MORE NOTES AND IT'S FINISHED—
TUM-TE-TE-TUM
HEY! YOU BIG ONION, YOU'VE RUINED ME-YOU'VE EATEN ALL MY MUSIC!

?
GOSH! I HAD NO IDEA IT WAS THAT BAD!
IT'S A HIGH CLASS PICCOLO, MAC GOOGAN, AND I'LL SELL IT VERY CHEAP!
BUT, AH DINNA WANT A PICCOLO — AH WANT A BAGPIPE —
OH, SO YOU WANT A BAGPIPE? WELL, STICK AROUND A MINUTE — I'LL BE BACK —
GUDE!
HELLO, MOE, WANT A PIECE F RUBBER TUBE, HOT WATER BOTTLE AND THAT OLD CHAIR —
AND BARGAINS I CAN GIVE YOU!
FIRST CLASS 2ND HAND DEALER
E-E-E-E-E-E-K!
HOOT MON!

A BULL-FIDDLE CASE IS A PRETTY HANDY THING IF YOU CAN JUST THINK OF SOMETHING TO DO WITH IT—
AND THESE GIVE ME A GREAT IDEA—
OH! HELLO, MINNIE — YOU'RE JUST IN TIME - I'VE GOT A SURPRISE FOR YOU—
OH, GOODY!
O-O-O-O-H! A YACHT!
ANCHORS AWEIGH!

MICKEY MOUSE
in
FORAY TO MOUNT FISHFLAKE
$1,000 TO ANY PARTY WHO CAN CLIMB TO THE SUMMIT OF MT. FISHFLAKE DURING THE WINTER. THIS DANGEROUS PEAK HAS NEVER BEEN SCALED EXCEPT IN THE SUMMER MONTHS. FOR SORE MUSCLES USE GAZOPP LINIMENT! ADV.
ZM 34-12-09
ARE Y' THINKIN' OF TRYIN' IT, HORACE?
ME CASH IN ON THAT THOUSAND! I COME O' MOUNTAINEER STOCK Y' KNOW--
IT'D BE EASY!
IT MUST BE A TOUGH CLIMB IF NOBODY EVER DID IT IN WINTER!
AS GUIDE, WE CAN'T FAIL!
MATCHES
I'LL BET MINNIE'LL WANT TO GO--SHE'S CRAZY OVER SNOW SPORTS!
HEY---- NO WOMEN! AND THAT'S FINAL!
THE VERY IDEA! A BODY'D THINK WE WERE MADE O' SUGAR--- A LITTLE HIKE IN THE SNOW WAS GOING TO MELT US--WHY---!
SUGAR? DON'T MAKE ME LAUGH!
A WOMAN CAN HIKE AS WELL AS ANY MAN AND---!
--AND A LOT BETTER N SOME I KNOW!
OH IS ZAT SO?
IF YOU GALS HAVE HAD ENOUGH, TURN BACK HERE! IT'LL BE TOO LATE ONCE WE GET INTO THEM MOUNTAIN FASTNESSES!
OH, DRY UP AND GIT ALONG!
HORACE! LOOK WHO'S HERE!
HIDDEN VALLEY
MT FISHFLAKE
HOWDY, FOLKS! GOIN' MY WAY?
NOW, LOOK HERE, DIPPY! YOU AIN'T IN ON OUR EXPEDITION--- BEAT IT. WILL YOU?
AIN'T NUTHIN' TO KEEP ME FRUM MOUNTAIN-CLIMBIN' SHOULD I WANTA-- IS THERE?
THAT'S RIGHT, HORACE! HE CAN GO ALONE, SO HE MIGHT AS WELL BE WITH US!
I'M S'POSED TO BE LEADER OF THIS CARAVAN AN' I GOT ABOUT AS MUCH SAY AS A - SON-IN-LAW!
HOURS PASS- QUITE A FEW OF 'EM! AND IT'S LUNCH-TIME!
ACCORDIN' TO MY COMPASS, TO REACH MT. FISHFLAKE FROM HERE, WE GO DUE NOR'-NOR'-EAST BY EAST FOR--!
LOOK OUT, HORACE! THE LEDGE'S BREAKIN'!
HALP!!
HANG ON--!
---WE GOTCHA!
THAT'S KEEPIN' YOUR HEAD IN A PINCH THE OLD HORSECOLLAR PRESENCE O' MIND! NOTICE I NEVER EVEN DROPPED THE PIE!
GREAT STUFF, HORACE! BUT HOW CAN WE USE THAT PIE FOR A COMPASS?
TO BE CONTINUED

MICKEY MOUSE
in
FORAY TO MOUNT FISHFLAKE
"WE'RE OUT TO TRY AN' CLIMB MT. FISHFLAKE! THERE'S A $1,000 PRIZE IN IT IF WE MAKE IT— AN' NOW HORACE HAS GONE AN' DROPPED OUR COMPASS OVER A CLIFF!"
DOGGONE IT, HORACE! WE'LL HAVE A HECK OF A TIME GETTIN' UP THERE WITHOUT A COMPASS!
DON'T GIVE IT A THOUGHT, M' BOY! I'M A REG'LAR HOMIN' PIGEON!
YEAH, BUT WE'RE NOT GOIN' HOME!
JUST LOOK! Y'CAN'T TELL ONE DIRECTION FROM ANOTHER!
OH, YES, I CAN! THE MOSS ON THE TREES ALLUS GROWS ON THE SOUTH SIDE!
SOUTH SIDE, RUBBISH! MY HOUSE FACES EAST AND ALL THE TREES IN THE FRONT YARD GOT MOSS ON 'EM!
WELL, I ALWAYS HEARD IT WAS THE NORTH — BUT I WISH WE HAD OUR COMPASS, JUST THE SAME!
IT'S GETTIN' PURTY STEEP! WE GOTTA BE ROPED TOGETHER, SO'S IF ONE SLIPS WE KIN HOLD HIM!
OR MAYBE TH' ONE THAT FALLS PULLS TH' REST DOWN!
WATCH WHAT YOU'RE DOIN'— YOU DON'T HAVE TO CHOKE ME!
GOODNESS! I HOPE HORACE KNOWS WHERE HE'S GOIN'!
WELL, I S'POSE IF WE KEEP GOIN' UP WE'LL GET THERE!
HEAVENLY DAY! DO YOU KNOW WHERE YOU'RE LEADING US?
ANY TIME I DON'T, I C'N ALWAYS ASK YOU!
GOSH! Y'CAN'T SEE TWO FEET AHEAD!
WOWW!!
HELP! HELP!
GOO' NIGHT! WHAT HAPPENED?
WHAT TH'?
EEEEEEEK!
GOSH!
HEY, HORACE! TIE THE END O' YOUR ROPE AROUND THAT ROCK AND CUT Y'SELF LOOSE— THAT'LL HOLD 'EM!
DON'T WORRY— WE'LL SAVE YA! JUST KEEP COOL!
DOGGONE! WE GOTTA FIGGER OUT SOME WAY TO SAVE 'EM!
YEAH! IT DON'T SEEM RIGHT TO LEAVE 'EM THERE!
FOR HEAVEN'S SAKE DO SOMETHING! WE'RE FREEZING!
I DON'T FEEL SO GOOD I DON'T!
OF ALL THE HALF-WITTED NINNIES— SITTIN' DOWN TO REST WHILE WE TURN INTO ICICLES— GET US OUT OF HERE THIS INSTANT!

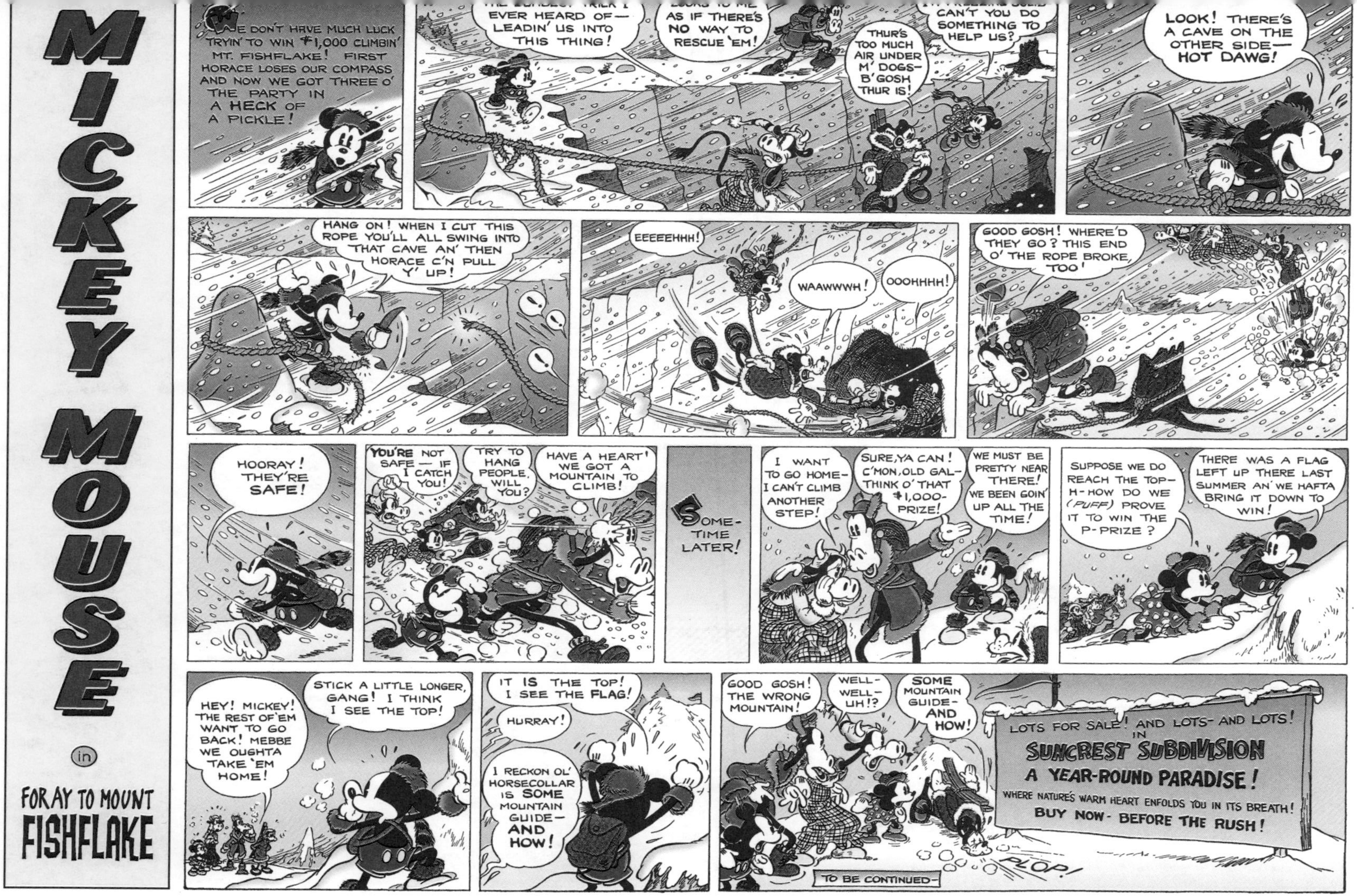
MICKEY MOUSE
in
FORAY TO MOUNT FISHFLAKE
WE DON'T HAVE MUCH LUCK TRYIN' TO WIN $1,000 CLIMBIN' MT. FISHFLAKE! FIRST HORACE LOSES OUR COMPASS AND NOW WE GOT THREE O' THE PARTY IN A HECK OF A PICKLE!
EVER HEARD OF— LEADIN' US INTO THIS THING!
AS IF THERE'S NO WAY TO RESCUE 'EM!
CAN'T YOU DO SOMETHING TO HELP US?
THUR'S TOO MUCH AIR UNDER M' DOGS— B' GOSH THUR IS!
LOOK! THERE'S A CAVE ON THE OTHER SIDE— HOT DAWG!
HANG ON! WHEN I CUT THIS ROPE YOU'LL ALL SWING INTO THAT CAVE AN' THEN HORACE C'N PULL Y' UP!
EEEEEHHH!
WAAWWWH!
OOOHHHH!
GOOD GOSH! WHERE'D THEY GO? THIS END O' THE ROPE BROKE, TOO!
HOORAY! THEY'RE SAFE!
YOU'RE NOT SAFE — IF I CATCH YOU!
TRY TO HANG PEOPLE, WILL YOU?
HAVE A HEART! WE GOT A MOUNTAIN TO CLIMB!
SOME-TIME LATER!
I WANT TO GO HOME— I CAN'T CLIMB ANOTHER STEP!
SURE, YA CAN! C'MON, OLD GAL— THINK O' THAT $1,000— PRIZE!
WE MUST BE PRETTY NEAR THERE! WE BEEN GOIN' UP ALL THE TIME!
SUPPOSE WE DO REACH THE TOP— H- HOW DO WE (PUFF) PROVE IT TO WIN THE P- PRIZE?
THERE WAS A FLAG LEFT UP THERE LAST SUMMER AN' WE HAFTA BRING IT DOWN TO WIN!
HEY! MICKEY! THE REST OF 'EM WANT TO GO BACK! MEBBE WE OUGHTA TAKE 'EM HOME!
STICK A LITTLE LONGER, GANG! I THINK I SEE THE TOP!
IT IS THE TOP! I SEE THE FLAG!
HURRAY!
I RECKON OL' HORSECOLLAR IS SOME MOUNTAIN GUIDE— AND HOW!
GOOD GOSH! THE WRONG MOUNTAIN!
WELL— WELL— UH!?
SOME MOUNTAIN GUIDE— AND HOW!
LOTS FOR SALE! AND LOTS- AND LOTS! IN SUNCREST SUBDIVISION A YEAR-ROUND PARADISE! WHERE NATURE'S WARM HEART ENFOLDS YOU IN ITS BREATH! BUY NOW - BEFORE THE RUSH!
PLOP!
TO BE CONTINUED—

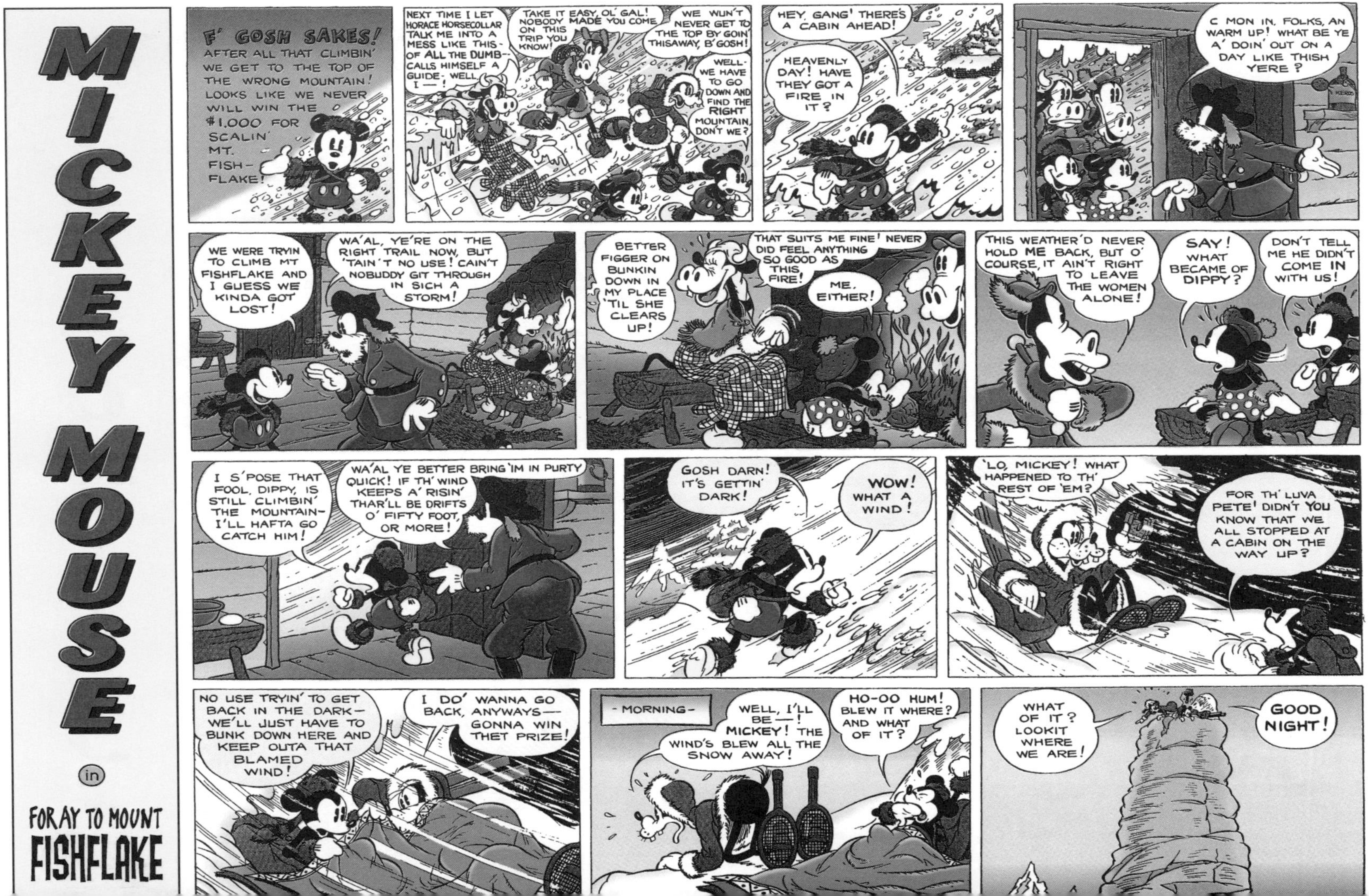
MICKEY MOUSE
in
FORAY TO MOUNT FISHFLAKE
F' GOSH SAKES! AFTER ALL THAT CLIMBIN' WE GET TO THE TOP OF THE WRONG MOUNTAIN! LOOKS LIKE WE NEVER WILL WIN THE $1,000 FOR SCALIN' MT. FISH-FLAKE!
NEXT TIME I LET HORACE HORSECOLLAR TALK ME INTO A MESS LIKE THIS - OF ALL THE DUMB-- CALLS HIMSELF A GUIDE - WELL, I — !
TAKE IT EASY, OL' GAL! NOBODY MADE YOU COME ON THIS TRIP YOU KNOW!
WE WUN'T NEVER GET TO THE TOP BY GOIN' THISAWAY, B'GOSH!
WELL - WE HAVE TO GO DOWN AND FIND THE RIGHT MOUNTAIN, DON'T WE?
HEY, GANG! THERE'S A CABIN AHEAD!
HEAVENLY DAY! HAVE THEY GOT A FIRE IN IT?
C MON IN, FOLKS, AN WARM UP! WHAT BE YE A' DOIN' OUT ON A DAY LIKE THISH YERE?
WE WERE TRYIN TO CLIMB MT FISHFLAKE AND I GUESS WE KINDA GOT LOST!
WA'AL, YE'RE ON THE RIGHT TRAIL NOW, BUT 'TAIN'T NO USE! CAIN'T NOBUDDY GIT THROUGH IN SICH A STORM!
BETTER FIGGER ON BUNKIN DOWN IN MY PLACE 'TIL SHE CLEARS UP!
THAT SUITS ME FINE! NEVER DID FEEL ANYTHING SO GOOD AS THIS FIRE!
ME, EITHER!
THIS WEATHER'D NEVER HOLD ME BACK, BUT O' COURSE, IT AIN'T RIGHT TO LEAVE THE WOMEN ALONE!
SAY! WHAT BECAME OF DIPPY?
DON'T TELL ME HE DIDN'T COME IN WITH US!
I S'POSE THAT FOOL, DIPPY, IS STILL CLIMBIN' THE MOUNTAIN - I'LL HAFTA GO CATCH HIM!
WA'AL YE BETTER BRING 'IM IN PURTY QUICK! IF TH' WIND KEEPS A' RISIN' THAR'LL BE DRIFTS O' FIFTY FOOT, OR MORE!
GOSH DARN! IT'S GETTIN' DARK!
WOW! WHAT A WIND!
'LO, MICKEY! WHAT HAPPENED TO TH' REST OF 'EM?
FOR TH' LUVA PETE! DIDN'T YOU KNOW THAT WE ALL STOPPED AT A CABIN ON THE WAY UP?
NO USE TRYIN' TO GET BACK IN THE DARK — WE'LL JUST HAVE TO BUNK DOWN HERE AND KEEP OUTA THAT BLAMED WIND!
I DO' WANNA GO BACK, ANYWAYS— GONNA WIN THET PRIZE!
- MORNING -
WELL, I'LL BE — ! MICKEY! THE WIND'S BLEW ALL THE SNOW AWAY!
HO-OO HUM! BLEW IT WHERE? AND WHAT OF IT?
WHAT OF IT? LOOKIT WHERE WE ARE!
GOOD NIGHT!

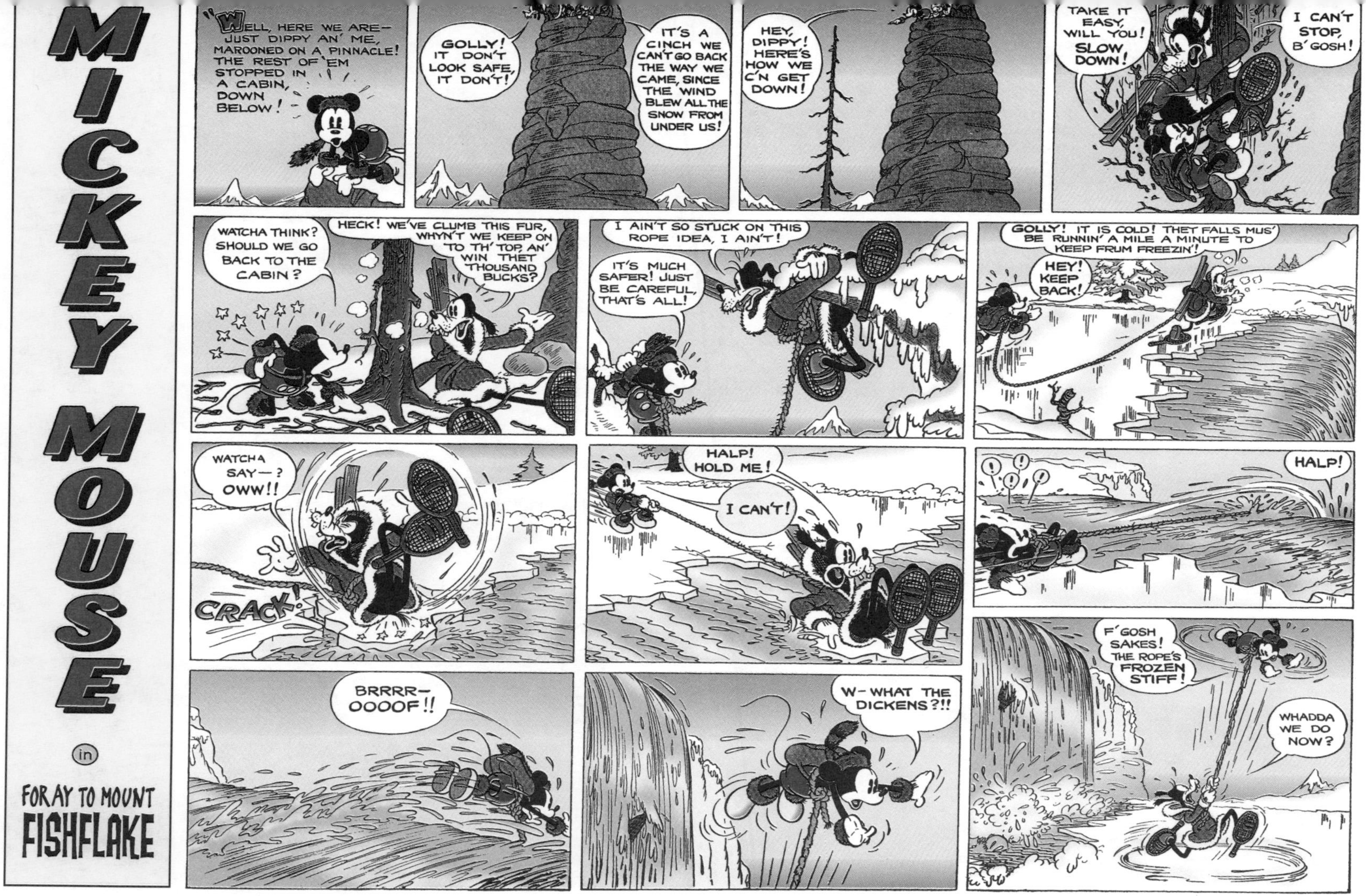
MICKEY MOUSE
in
FORAY TO MOUNT
FISHFLAKE
"WELL, HERE WE ARE— JUST DIPPY AN' ME, MAROONED ON A PINNACLE! THE REST OF 'EM STOPPED IN A CABIN, DOWN BELOW!
GOLLY! IT DON'T LOOK SAFE, IT DON'T!
IT'S A CINCH WE CAN'T GO BACK THE WAY WE CAME, SINCE THE WIND BLEW ALL THE SNOW FROM UNDER US!
HEY, DIPPY! HERE'S HOW WE C'N GET DOWN!
TAKE IT EASY, WILL YOU! SLOW DOWN!
I CAN'T STOP, B'GOSH!
WATCHA THINK? SHOULD WE GO BACK TO THE CABIN?
HECK! WE'VE CLUMB THIS FUR, WHYN'T WE KEEP ON TO TH' TOP, AN' WIN THET THOUSAND BUCKS?
I AIN'T SO STUCK ON THIS ROPE IDEA, I AIN'T!
IT'S MUCH SAFER! JUST BE CAREFUL, THAT'S ALL!
GOLLY! IT IS COLD! THET FALLS MUS' BE RUNNIN' A MILE A MINUTE TO KEEP FRUM FREEZIN'!
HEY! KEEP BACK!
WATCHA SAY—? OWW!!
CRACK!
HALP! HOLD ME!
I CAN'T!
HALP!
BRRRR— OOOOF!!
W—WHAT THE DICKENS?!!
F'GOSH SAKES! THE ROPE'S FROZEN STIFF!
WHADDA WE DO NOW?

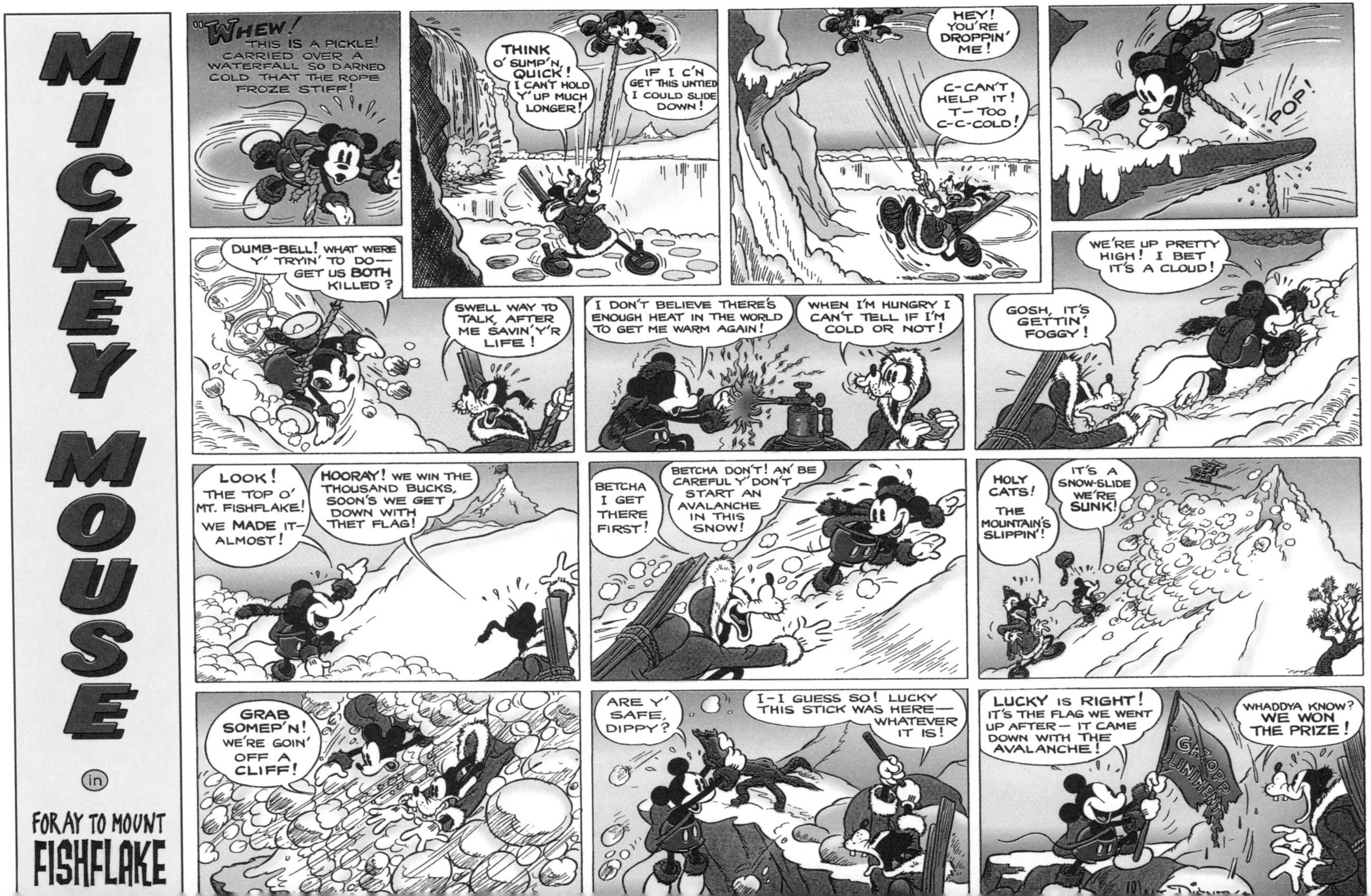
MICKEY MOUSE
in
FORAY TO MOUNT FISHFLAKE
"WHEW! THIS IS A PICKLE! CARRIED OVER A WATERFALL SO DARNED COLD THAT THE ROPE FROZE STIFF!
THINK O' SUMP'N, QUICK! I CAN'T HOLD Y' UP MUCH LONGER!
IF I C'N GET THIS UNTIED I COULD SLIDE DOWN!
HEY! YOU'RE DROPPIN' ME!
C-CAN'T HELP IT! T-TOO C-C-COLD!
POP!
DUMB-BELL! WHAT WERE Y' TRYIN' TO DO— GET US BOTH KILLED?
SWELL WAY TO TALK, AFTER ME SAVIN' Y'R LIFE!
I DON'T BELIEVE THERE'S ENOUGH HEAT IN THE WORLD TO GET ME WARM AGAIN!
WHEN I'M HUNGRY I CAN'T TELL IF I'M COLD OR NOT!
GOSH, IT'S GETTIN' FOGGY!
WE'RE UP PRETTY HIGH! I BET IT'S A CLOUD!
LOOK! THE TOP O' MT. FISHFLAKE! WE MADE IT— ALMOST!
HOORAY! WE WIN THE THOUSAND BUCKS, SOON'S WE GET DOWN WITH THET FLAG!
BETCHA I GET THERE FIRST!
BETCHA DON'T! AN' BE CAREFUL Y' DON'T START AN AVALANCHE IN THIS SNOW!
HOLY CATS! THE MOUNTAIN'S SLIPPIN'!
IT'S A SNOW-SLIDE WE'RE SUNK!
GRAB SOMEP'N! WE'RE GOIN' OFF A CLIFF!
ARE Y' SAFE, DIPPY?
I-I GUESS SO! LUCKY THIS STICK WAS HERE— WHATEVER IT IS!
LUCKY IS RIGHT! IT'S THE FLAG WE WENT UP AFTER— IT CAME DOWN WITH THE AVALANCHE!
GAZOPP LINIMENT
WHADDYA KNOW? WE WON THE PRIZE!

MICKEY MOUSE
in
FORAY TO MOUNT FISHFLAKE
FOLKS — THE FLAG ON MT. FISHFLAKE! NOW, ALL WE HAFTA DO IS GET DOWN AND CLAIM THE $1,000 PRIZE!
WE HAD A SLED, WE COULD GET DOWN IN A HURRY!
OF M' OWN! YA SEE WHUT LITTLE SPACE THEY TAKE! LOTS BETTER'N CARRYIN' LONG, AWKWARD THINGS!
THEY WON'T WORK—— THEY'RE TOO FLOPSY!
A' CARRYIN' FASTEN ON TOP AND HOLD 'EM STRAIGHT!
CABIN AHOY!
IT'S MICKEY!
THEY'VE GOT THE FLAG!
HOORAY!
NEXT DAY! THE HAPPY PARTY IS NOW LEAVING THE OFFICES OF THE GAZOPP LINIMENT CO. WITH THE HARD-EARNED PRIZE!
JUST A MOMENT, FOLKS! BEFORE YOU SPEND YOUR MONEY FOOLISHLY, LET ME SEND UP A DOZEN CASES O' LINIMENT TO EACH HOUSE. IT'S ONLY $10 A CASE AND YOU'LL BE PROTECTED AGAINST—!
NO, THANK YOU, WE NEVER USE IT!
MERCY! WASN'T THAT SALESMAN A PEST!
NEVER HEARD SO MUCH BLATHERIN' IN MY LIFE!
BUT, SAY— WHAT ARE WE GOIN' TO DO WITH THE PRIZE?
HOWDY-DO, BROTHER! HOWJA LIKE TO INVEST IN TEN SHARES O' GILT-EDGED STOCK, ONLY A HUN'ERD DOLLARS A SHARE?
IN WHAT COMPANY?
THE GAZOPP LINIMENT CO., LTD! THE SAFEST———!
NO, THANK YOU!
MY GOSH! THEY'RE WORKIN' HARD TO GET THEIR MONEY BACK!
RECKON THEY NEVER FIGGERED ANYBUDDY TO WIN IT!
THEY DIDN'T KNOW US!
I THINK WE SHOULD GIVE IT TO SOME GOOD CHARITY! IF WE LEAVE IT TO THE MEN, THERE'S NO TELLIN' WHAT THEY'LL DO!
YOU'RE DEAD RIGHT, MINNIE! WE'LL JUST PUT OUR FOOT DOWN! WHY, IF HORACE HAD HIS WAY—!
JUST LIKE A WOMAN'S IDEA! NOW IF YOU'D LET ME INVEST IT, WE'D ALL MAKE SOMETHIN'!
OHO! WHAT'D I TELL YOU?
NOW THESE BONDS—!
GAZOPP?
IN A WAY, YES! THE GAZOPP FOUNDATION FOR THRONELESS KINGS, A MOST WORTHY AND ———!
NO!
SLAM!
HELLO, MR. GAZOPP? THIS IS MICKEY MOUSE! PLEASE TELL YOUR SALESMEN TO CALL AT THE ORPHANS' HOME — WE JUST GAVE OUR PRIZE MONEY TO THEM! GOOD-BYE!
The End

SCOUTMASTER MICKEY:-
"NOW TROOPER GOOFY, I WANT TO TEST YOUR KNOWLEDGE OF THE COMPASS. YOU ARE FACING THE RISING SUN. ON YOUR LEFT IS THE NORTH. WHAT IS BEHIND YOU ?"
GOOFY :-
"THAT'S MY LUNCH !"
SCOUTMASTER MICKEY:-
"THIS TEA TASTES LIKE VINEGAR !"
GOOFY:-
"THEN I MUST HAVE MADE IT WITH COFFEE. I KEEP THE TEA IN THE BATH SALTS BOTTLE !"

DONALD DUCK
by WALT DISNEY
DONALD DUCK HOLLYWOOD CALIF.
ZS 37-10-17
Dear Donald:
I am sending your angel nephews, Louie, Huey and Dewey, to stay with you while their father is in the hospital.
A giant firecracker exploded under his chair. The little darlings are SO playful. I hope you enjoy them.
Your cousin, Della.
KNOCK! KNOCK!!
HELLO! UNCA DONALD!

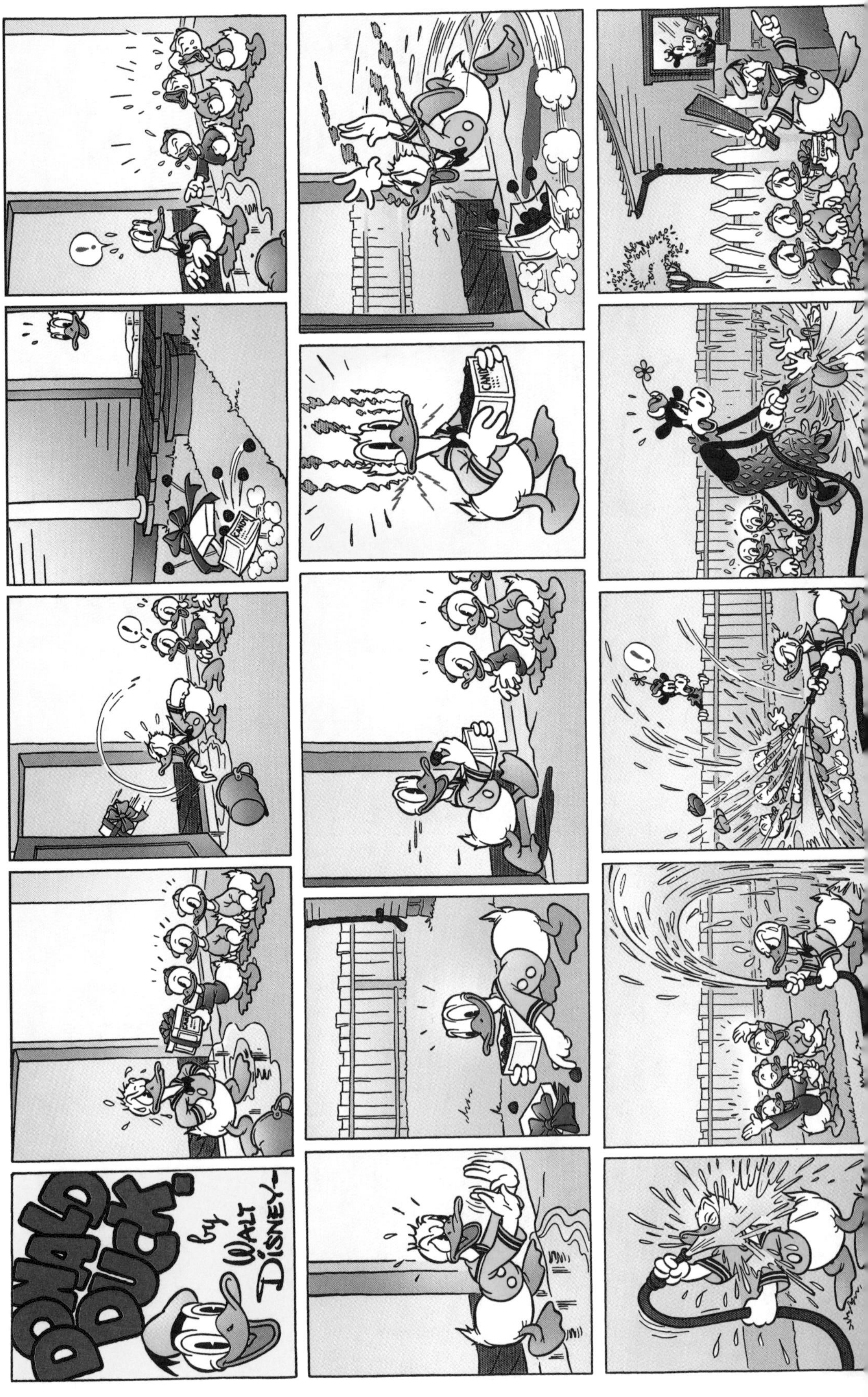
DONALD DUCK
by WALT DISNEY
CANDY

DONALD DUCK
by WALT DISNEY
HI, DONALD HOW'S YER NEPHEWS?
!
SO!! HIDING!
HELLO, UNCA DONALD!
!
QUACK QUACK QUACK QUACK !!!!

DONALD DUCK.
by
WALT DISNEY
URK!
?
?
CRASH!
SO!

DONALD DUCK
by WALT DISNEY
CRASH!!
!
?
?
?
!
!
CRASH!
BREAK MY WINDOWS, WILL YOU?

DONALD DUCK.
by WALT DISNEY
WHONG
RING!
?
!
TELEGRAM FOR YOU, UNCA DONALD!
!
IT'S FROM YOUR MA! SHE WANTS YOU TO COME BACK HOME!
WAAAAAAA! WE WANT TO STAY HERE! WE DON'T WANNA GO HOME!
OH! YOU DON'T, DON'TCHA?

WALT DISNEY'S
GREMLINS
W WDC 35-15

GREMLIN CUT OUT
"THE FIFINELLA"

BUCKY BUG
by WALT DISNEY
THERE'S NOT MUCH DOING IN THE NEWS! I THINK I'LL TAKE A LITTLE SNOOZE!
HO HUM! I'M SLEEPY!!
W WDC 58-03
RAP RAP RAP
NOW WHO'S THAT BREAKIN' UP MY NAP?
IT'S BO! SAY, CUT THAT RACKET OUT... AND TELL ME WHAT'S THE FUSS ABOUT!!
COME ON, KID! QUICK!! SEE WHAT I'VE FOUND!!
THE THING WAS SAILIN' NEAR THE GROUND! QUICK AS A FLASH I GRABBED THE ROPE, AND TIED IT FAST! IT'S SAFE... I HOPE!
WHAT'S SAFE?
YOU'LL SEE! WE'LL BE THERE SOON!
THERE 'TIS!
GEE WHIZ! A BIG BALLOON!!
IT'S PRETTY, BO ... AND BIG .... BUT, SAY.... WHAT'S THE THING GOOD FOR, ANYWAY ??????
I'VE BEEN A TRAMP, FOOTLOOSE AND FREE! I'VE TRAVELED OVER LAND AND SEA!! BUT THERE IS ONLY ONE PLACE WHERE I'VE NEVER TRAVELED... THAT'S THE AIR!!
NOW LISTEN, KID... AND PAY ATTENTION!!
WILL YOU JOIN MY BALLOON ASCENSION?

I THINK THAT FLYING WOULD BE GREAT... BUT FRANKLY, BO, I HESITATE TO TRAVEL, DANGLING FROM THAT THING ON JUST THIS FLIMSY BIT OF STRING! !!!
SHUCKS, SON! IN JUST A LITTLE WHILE I'LL FIX IT SO'S WE'LL FLY IN STYLE!!!
BUT HOW?
WELL, BUCKY, SINCE YOU ASK IT... ... WE'LL NEED SOME ROPE.. ... WE'LL NEED A BASKET!!
WE'LL FIND THE STUFF, WITHOUT A DOUBT, IN ALL THIS JUNK THAT'S STREWN ABOUT!!
WHAT DID I TELL YOU? HERE'S A FIND!! AN ALMOST BRAND-NEW LEMON RIND!!
A LEMON RIND!! WHAT FOR???
YOU DOPE!!
JUST NEVER MIND... AND FIND SOME ROPE!
I FOUND SOME ROPE, BO. ... QUITE A LOT!! BUT I CAN'T MOVE IT FROM THIS SPOT!
THERE'S MILES OF IT... MORE THAN ENOUGH!!
BUT HOW'LL WE MOVE THIS HEAVY STUFF!!
YOU SEE THAT, HORSE FLY WAND'RIN' LOOSE? JUST WATCH ME CATCH HIM WITH THIS NOOSE!! WE'LL HARNESS HIM! HE'LL HAUL AROUND THE LEMON RIND AND ROPE WE'VE FOUND!!

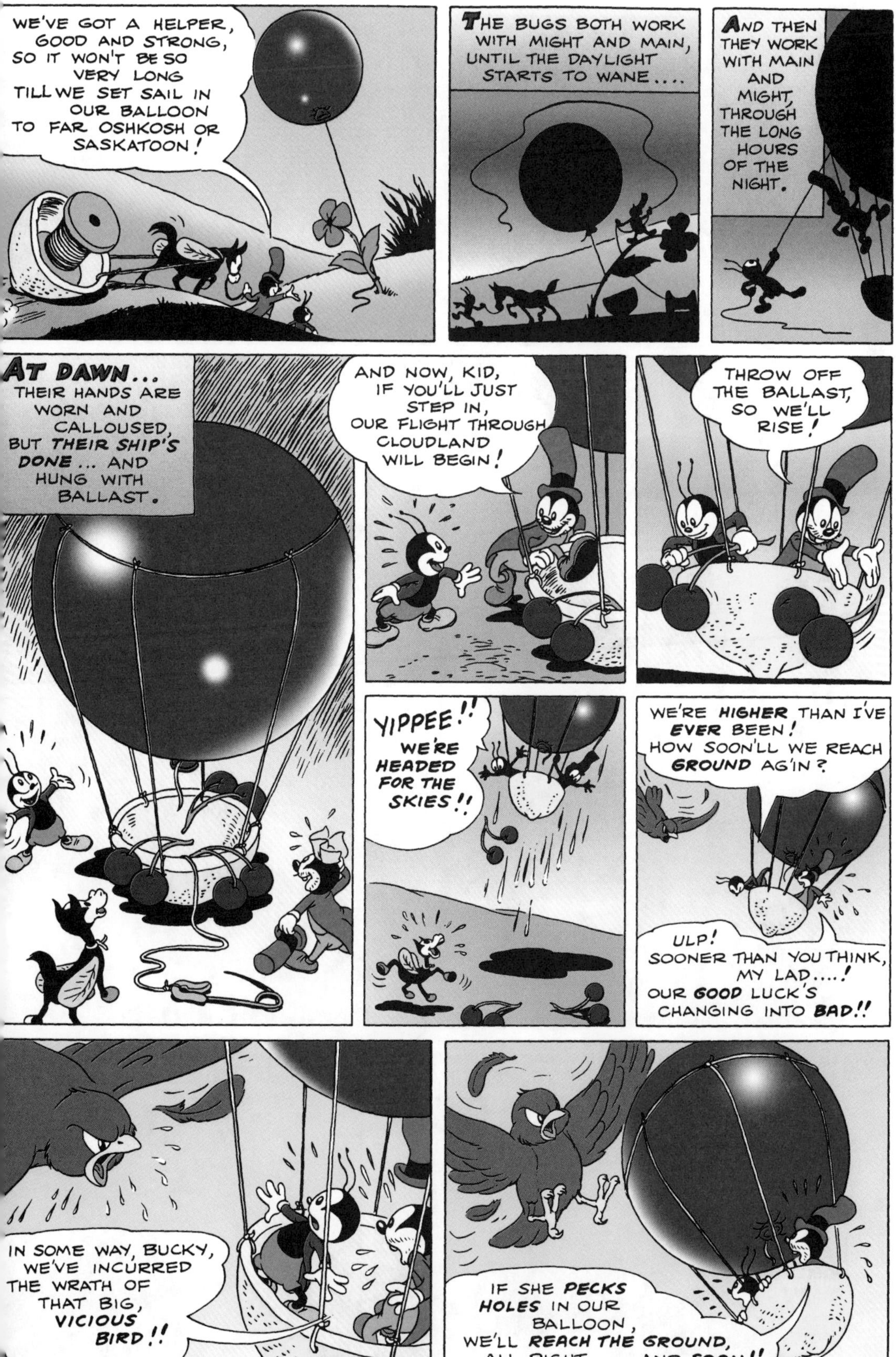
WE'VE GOT A HELPER, GOOD AND STRONG, SO IT WON'T BE SO VERY LONG TILL WE SET SAIL IN OUR BALLOON TO FAR OSHKOSH OR SASKATOON!
THE BUGS BOTH WORK WITH MIGHT AND MAIN, UNTIL THE DAYLIGHT STARTS TO WANE....
AND THEN THEY WORK WITH MAIN AND MIGHT, THROUGH THE LONG HOURS OF THE NIGHT.
AT DAWN... THEIR HANDS ARE WORN AND CALLOUSED, BUT THEIR SHIP'S DONE... AND HUNG WITH BALLAST.
AND NOW, KID, IF YOU'LL JUST STEP IN, OUR FLIGHT THROUGH CLOUDLAND WILL BEGIN!
THROW OFF THE BALLAST, SO WE'LL RISE!
YIPPEE!! WE'RE HEADED FOR THE SKIES!!
WE'RE HIGHER THAN I'VE EVER BEEN! HOW SOON'LL WE REACH GROUND AG'IN?
ULP! SOONER THAN YOU THINK, MY LAD....! OUR GOOD LUCK'S CHANGING INTO BAD!!
IN SOME WAY, BUCKY, WE'VE INCURRED THE WRATH OF THAT BIG, VICIOUS BIRD!!
IF SHE PECKS HOLES IN OUR BALLOON, WE'LL REACH THE GROUND, ALL RIGHT .... AND SOON!!

LOOK, BO! WE'RE PASSING O'ER A TREE!!
QUICK! HAND THAT ANCHOR ROPE TO ME!
JUST CROSS YOUR FINGERS, KID, AND HOPE THAT I CAN CATCH ON WITH THIS ROPE!
I CAUGHT IT! QUICK, NOW.. ... FOLLOW ME.... AND WE'LL JUMP DOWN TO SAFETY!!
BUT BOTH BUGS MISS THE BRANCH.. .... AND, GEE!... KEEP RIGHT ON FALLING THROUGH THE TREE!
BUT NOW THEIR FLIGHT COMES TO A STOP! THEY LAND ON SOMETHING SOFT......
KERPLOP
WELL, LOOKIT, BO! NOW WHO'D HAVE GUESSED WE'D WIND UP IN THAT OLD BIRD'S NEST?!!
GREAT JUMPIN' JEEPERS!! I DON'T YEARN TO BE FOUND HERE ON HER RETURN!
SHE'D EAT US UP, I BETCHA!!
WOW!! RUN FOR YOUR LIFE! HERE SHE COMES NOW!!

THANK GOODNESS THAT THIS TREE IS **HOLLOW**!! JUMP RIGHT IN, BUCKY ... AND I'LL FOLLOW!
WE'RE TRAPPED, BO! WITH THAT **BIRD** ON GUARD, THE ONLY ENTRANCE NOW IS **BARRED**!
I'M NOT SO SURE! I THINK I SEE **ANOTHER HOLLOW** IN THE TREE!
A **HOLLOW BRANCH**!! PERHAPS THROUGH THERE WE SOON CAN REACH THE OUTER AIR!
SO THROUGH THE HOLLOW BRANCH THEY CRAWL..
THIS MAY NOT LEAD US OUT AT ALL!
YEP, BO! JUST LOOK! YOUR GUESS WAS RIGHT...
.... 'CAUSE WAY UP THERE I SEE A **LIGHT**!!
HURRAY, BO! HERE WE'RE **SAFE AT LAST**, FOR ALL OUR FORMER DANGER'S PAST!
GEE, BO! I'M TANGLED IN THESE **ROPES**!!
SO'M I! GOSH, WE'RE A PAIR OF DOPES! WE'RE **WORSE OFF** THAN WE'VE **EVER** BEEN ...!!!
THIS IS A SPIDER'S WEB WE'RE IN!!!
NOW LOOK WOT YOU TWO GUYS HAVE DONE! YOU'VE **ROONED** THE BIGGEST WEB I'VE SPUN!!
IT TOOK **ALL AFTERNOON** TO SPIN!! AN' **NOW** LOOK AT THE SHAPE IT'S IN!!

YOU TORE IT! NOW IT HANGS IN RUINS! I SPUN DAT WEB TO CATCH BALLOONS!!
BALLOONS?
YUP! JUST DIS MORNIN', I SAW A GREAT, BIG ONE SAILIN' BY! IT'S ALLUS BEEN ME LIFE'S AMBITION TO FLY IN ONE!
THEN STOP YOUR WISHIN'! THAT'S OUR BALLOON.. ...TIED TO THIS TREE!
IT'S YOURS.. ... IF YOU'LL HELP BO AND ME!
THE BUGS' BALLOON SOON GOES TO TRADE FOR PARACHUTES THE SPIDER'S MADE.
DEY'RE FINISHED!
THANKS! NOW WE CAN GO!
T'ANKS FOR DE B'LOON!
GERONIMO!!
I'M GLAD WE GOT AWAY SO QUICK FROM THAT BIG, DUMB BALLOONATIC! HE COULD HAVE EATEN US, INSTEAD, BUT THOUGHTS OF FLYING FILLED HIS HEAD!
WELL, BO, THAT SPIDER MIGHT LIKE FLYING, BUT, AS FOR US, THERE'S NO DENYING...
...WE'RE THROUGH WITH IT! WE'VE HAD OUR SHARE OF TRAV'LING IN THE UPPER AIR!!
I THINK, OLD PAL, THAT YOU HAVE FOUND THERE'S NOTHING LIKE GOOD, SOLID GROUND!!

JOSÉ (JOE) CARIOCA
by
WALT DISNEY
SHE BEAUTIFUL!
RIO DAILY
HEDDY AMOUR
AMERICAN MOVIE STAR ARRIVES TODAY AT AIRPORT
OF MINE! I MUST GO SEE HER.
USE NO GANCHOS
TAKE A STREET CAR TOGATHER! MAYBE I CAN GET HER AUTOGRAPH!
HUH! GULP! LOOK, CARLOS! I NEVER RIDE THE STREET CAR...NOTHING BOT TAXIS. SO RON ALONG!
TAXI? DON' MAKE ME LAUGH! IF YOU TOOK A TAXI, YOU COULDN'T AFFORD TO EAT FOR A WEEK! I'LL BET YOU'RE GOING TO HEETCH-HIKE!
AIRPORT
BESIDES, I BET YOU DON' EVEN KNOW HER!
CAR STOP
STOP
HE WAS RIGHT, AND EEF HE KNEW EET, HE'D MAKE ME THE LAUGHING-STOCK OF THE TOWN! BESIDES, I DON' KNOW THEES GORL!
AH! A CAR STOPPING FOR ME!
HERE YOU ARE, FALLOW, RIGHT AT THE AIRPORT!
ULP! AN' THERE'S CARLOS. EEF HE SEES ME, I'M DONE FOR.
OH, OH! A CAB PARKED NEAR HIM! MAYBE I CAN SNEAK EEN WAN DOOR AN' OUT THE OTHER!
JOSÉ! YOU DEED TAKE A TAXI...I'M SORRY FOR THE REMARKS I MADE! I...I.
OF COURSE, I TOOK A CAB! DEEDN'T YOU SEE ME STEP OUT OF EET?
HMM!
I SORTAINLY DEED!
AND YOU OWE ME TWO CONTOS! ALL THE WAY FROM OP TOWN! REMEMBER?
HEH! OF COURSE! HEH!
ZS 44-09-10

JOSÉ (JOE) CARIOCA
by
WALT DISNEY
SO THEES MOVIE STAR ARRIVING HERE AT THE AIRPORT EEZ AN OL' GORL FRAN', EH? WELL, I DON' BELIEVE EET!
GATE
ALWAYS YOU TOL' OS FALLOWS WHAT A BEEG SHOTS YOU ARE! NOW I'LL FIND OUT FOR SURE!
WHAT WEEL I DO? HE'LL MAKE ME THE LAUGHING-STOCK OF RIO!
WHAT'S THE MATTER, JOSÉ? YOU ACT NERVOUS, HEH!
I'VE GOT TO THEENK OF SOMETHEENG!
AH!
I'LL BE RIGHT BACK!
WOW! WHAT FON! TOO BAD YOU FALLOWS HAVE TO WORK...
PORTERS' STATION
SI? WHY?
TONI, THE OWNER OF LUCIA'S OPTOWN CAFE, EEZ GEEVING AWAY ALL THE GRAPEJUICE YOU CAN DREENK! HE'S A NEW PAPA!
HUH!
OUT OF OUR WAY!
PORTERS' STATION
ZIP
ZIP
FLIGHT FIVE NOW COMING IN AT GATE THREE.
THAT'S HER PLANE, JOSÉ!
SO EET EEZ!
GULP! HE...HE'S WEETH HER!
HERE'S A TIP FOR CARRYING MY BAGS, SON, AND THANK YOU!
MNX25¢
The End

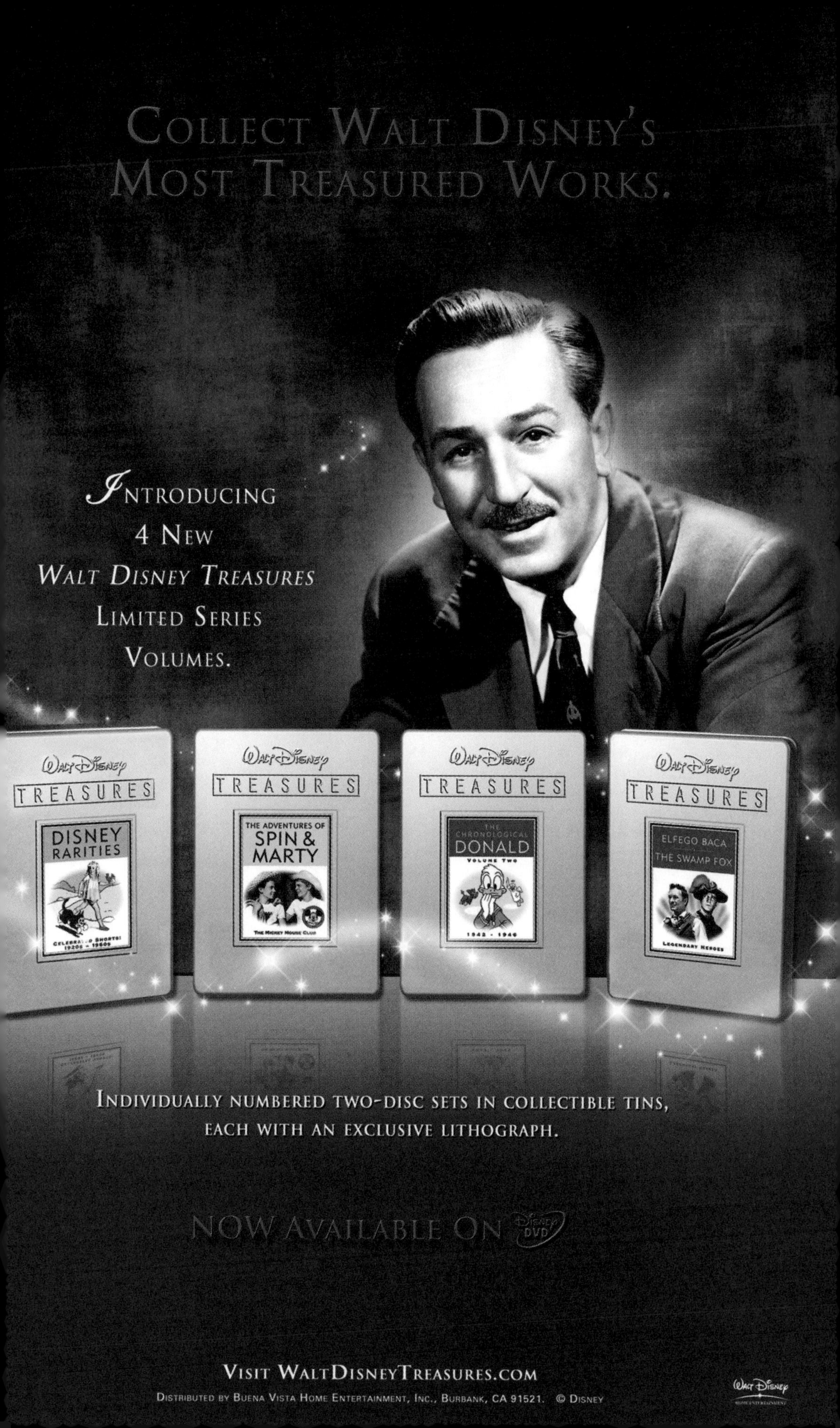
Collect Walt Disney's
Most Treasured Works.
Introducing
4 New
Walt Disney Treasures
Limited Series
Volumes.
Walt Disney Treasures
Disney Rarities
Walt Disney Treasures
The Adventures of Spin & Marty
The Mickey Mouse Club
Walt Disney Treasures
The Chronological Donald
Volume Two
1942 - 1946
Walt Disney Treasures
Elfego Baca
The Swamp Fox
Legendary Heroes
Individually numbered two-disc sets in collectible tins,
each with an exclusive lithograph.
Now Available On Disney DVD
Visit WaltDisneyTreasures.com
Distributed by Buena Vista Home Entertainment, Inc., Burbank, CA 91521. © Disney
Walt Disney Home Entertainment

A CLOSER LOOK AT *THE MONEY MINT* AND *RACE TO THE SOUTH SEAS*

by David Gerstein

Disney comics have always been products of their time—but never more so than in their early days. Everything from the vintage stories' visual milieu to their cultural references bespoke prewar small-town America; or, more precisely, the way small-town America perceived itself, however divorced from reality such perceptions may have been. Characters' language reflected the era: a wallet was also called a "billfold" and shopping was "marketing." Expressions like "by gollies," "doggone it," and "for gosh sakes" were commonplace.

And then there was the Other: the way in which prewar pop culture represented those who came from groups outside America's white, semi-gentrified majority. Comics, films, and fiction at the time were all loaded with broadly caricatured, presumed humorous images of Africans, Asians, poor whites, Italians, and others "not like us," and Disney comics were not immune to the trend. For example, Disney characters from the Deep South—the allegorically African-American Brer Rabbit and white Brer Fox and Hard Haid Moe—spoke in thicker countrified dialect than they do today, while in Carl Barks' "Race to the South Seas," island natives were presented as primitives, some speaking educated English but others utilizing pidgin.

Before condemning these stories' creators, however, we need to take several factors into account. In comics' golden age, the use of ethnic and regional caricatures was not necessarily intended as hurtful. Stereotypes were seen by many as a natural element of humoristic shorthand—they were "what you used," as a creator of fiction, when you wanted to create quick laughs or add local color with minimal effort. So second-nature were these clichés, in fact, that the comics community's outspoken supporters of civil rights—notably Walt Kelly and Theodor "Dr. Seuss" Geisel—could casually employ them, too, without pausing to think about their impact.

The exact nature of this impact, admittedly, is open to debate. A forward-thinking 1940s reader might have laughed at an eccentric, hayseedlike black character no differently than at a white hayseed—"they come in all colors," so to speak—and not let it affect his interactions with real-life African-Americans. Many minority audiences, too, took the era's negative stereotypes in stride. But it cannot be disputed that closed-minded individuals used negative stereotypes to bolster their prejudices, or that the general absence of positive stereotypes stood as a demoralizing factor for minorities.

This is not to say that Disney comics themselves were wanting for positive stereotypes. To their credit, Carl Barks, Floyd Gottfredson and others did try to strike blows for the oppressed, regardless of how minorities were otherwise portrayed. In "South Seas," for example, the island natives aren't dumb; some wise up to Gladstone's exploitation of them, while others' seeming fealty to Scrooge is revealed as a put-on for which they've been financially compensated. In Gottfredson's "Mickey Mouse Sails for Treasure Island" (not included in this volume), Mickey battles alongside a native tribe against explicitly white bad guys. And of course, Brer Rabbit forever outsmarts Brer Fox.

We hope you will look at "The Money Mint," "Race to the South Seas," and similar stories in *Walt Disney Treasures* as relics of their less enlightened time. We present the stories here in the interest of preserving their more enduring positive attributes for posterity—even if it means presenting history "warts and all."

— *David Gerstein*

Old-time Disney comics invoke ethnic and regional stereotypes—even as they mock Western culture for its faith in those stereotypes. In this example from "In Search of Jungle Treasure" *(1937—not included in this volume), Goofy bears the brunt of the joke for his presumption that rural Africans should be uneducated.*

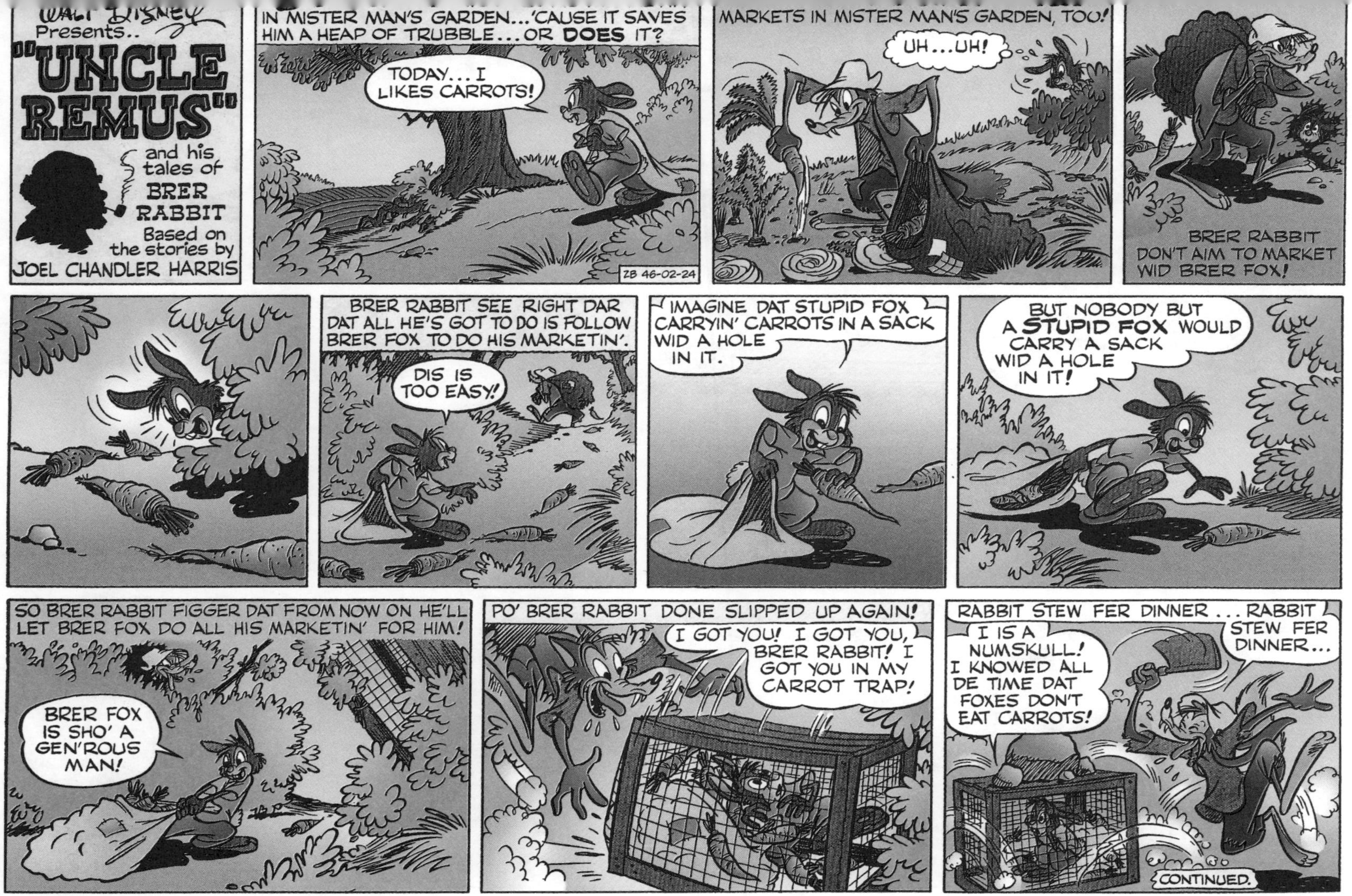
Walt Disney Presents..
"UNCLE REMUS"
and his tales of BRER RABBIT
Based on the stories by JOEL CHANDLER HARRIS
IN MISTER MAN'S GARDEN...'CAUSE IT SAVES HIM A HEAP OF TRUBBLE...OR **DOES** IT?
TODAY... I LIKES CARROTS!
ZB 46-02-24
MARKETS IN MISTER MAN'S GARDEN, TOO!
UH...UH!
BRER RABBIT DON'T AIM TO MARKET WID BRER FOX!
BRER RABBIT SEE RIGHT DAR DAT ALL HE'S GOT TO DO IS FOLLOW BRER FOX TO DO HIS MARKETIN'.
DIS IS TOO EASY!
IMAGINE DAT STUPID FOX CARRYIN' CARROTS IN A SACK WID A HOLE IN IT.
BUT NOBODY BUT A **STUPID FOX** WOULD CARRY A SACK WID A HOLE IN IT!
SO BRER RABBIT FIGGER DAT FROM NOW ON HE'LL LET BRER FOX DO ALL HIS MARKETIN' FOR HIM!
BRER FOX IS SHO' A GEN'ROUS MAN!
PO' BRER RABBIT DONE SLIPPED UP AGAIN!
I GOT YOU! I GOT YOU, BRER RABBIT! I GOT YOU IN MY CARROT TRAP!
RABBIT STEW FER DINNER ... RABBIT STEW FER DINNER...
I IS A NUMSKULL! I KNOWED ALL DE TIME DAT FOXES DON'T EAT CARROTS!
CONTINUED.

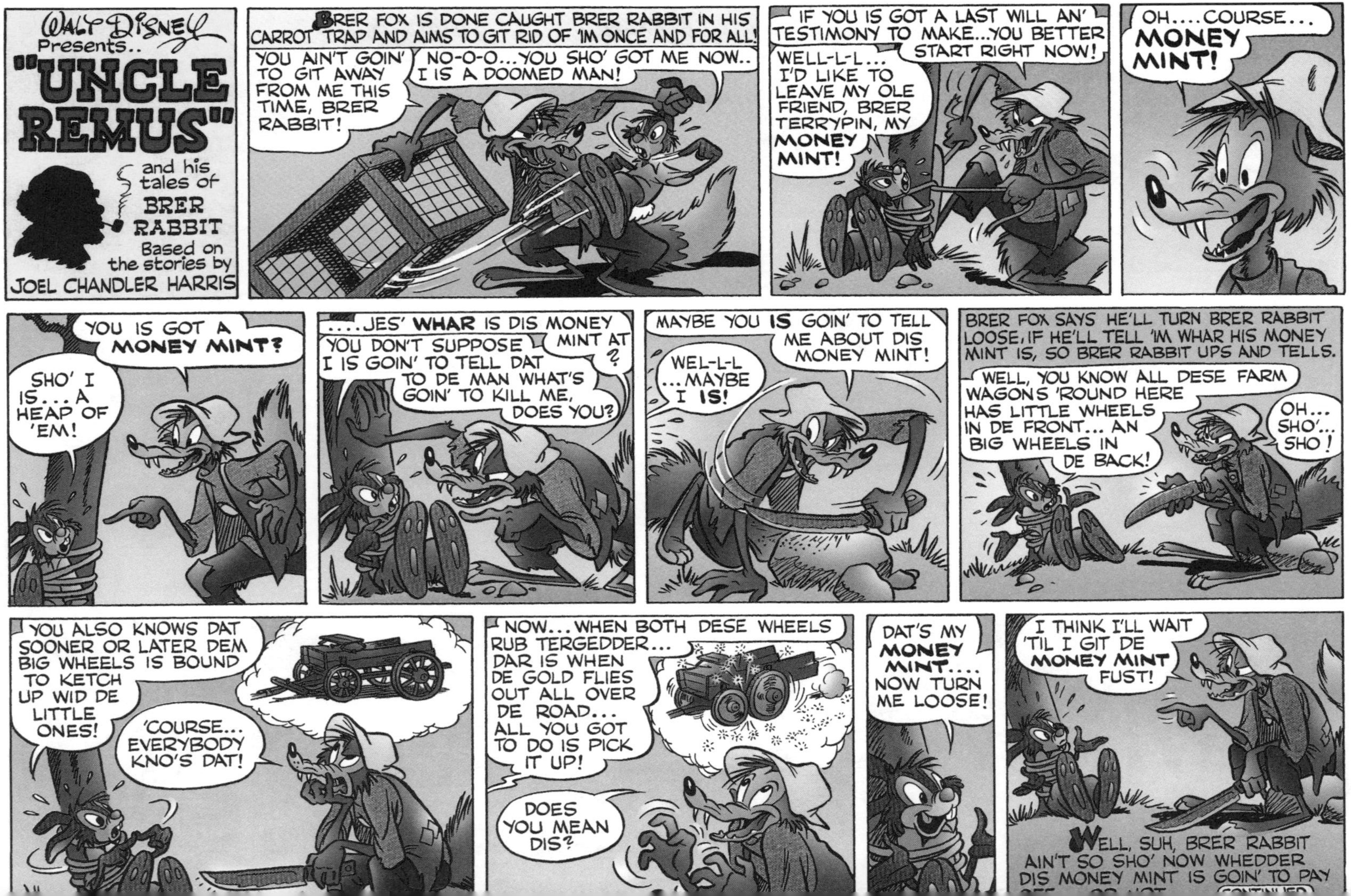
Walt Disney Presents.. "UNCLE REMUS" and his tales of BRER RABBIT
Based on the stories by JOEL CHANDLER HARRIS
BRER FOX IS DONE CAUGHT BRER RABBIT IN HIS CARROT TRAP AND AIMS TO GIT RID OF 'IM ONCE AND FOR ALL!
YOU AIN'T GOIN' TO GIT AWAY FROM ME THIS TIME, BRER RABBIT!
NO-O-O...YOU SHO' GOT ME NOW.. I IS A DOOMED MAN!
IF YOU IS GOT A LAST WILL AN' TESTIMONY TO MAKE...YOU BETTER START RIGHT NOW!
WELL-L-L... I'D LIKE TO LEAVE MY OLE FRIEND, BRER TERRYPIN, MY MONEY MINT!
OH....COURSE... MONEY MINT!
YOU IS GOT A MONEY MINT?
SHO' I IS...A HEAP OF 'EM!
....JES' WHAR IS DIS MONEY MINT AT?
YOU DON'T SUPPOSE I IS GOIN' TO TELL DAT TO DE MAN WHAT'S GOIN' TO KILL ME, DOES YOU?
MAYBE YOU IS GOIN' TO TELL ME ABOUT DIS MONEY MINT!
WEL-L-L ...MAYBE I IS!
BRER FOX SAYS HE'LL TURN BRER RABBIT LOOSE, IF HE'LL TELL 'IM WHAR HIS MONEY MINT IS, SO BRER RABBIT UPS AND TELLS.
WELL, YOU KNOW ALL DESE FARM WAGONS 'ROUND HERE HAS LITTLE WHEELS IN DE FRONT... AN BIG WHEELS IN DE BACK!
OH... SHO'... SHO!
YOU ALSO KNOWS DAT SOONER OR LATER DEM BIG WHEELS IS BOUND TO KETCH UP WID DE LITTLE ONES!
'COURSE... EVERYBODY KNO'S DAT!
NOW...WHEN BOTH DESE WHEELS RUB TERGEDDER... DAR IS WHEN DE GOLD FLIES OUT ALL OVER DE ROAD... ALL YOU GOT TO DO IS PICK IT UP!
DOES YOU MEAN DIS?
DAT'S MY MONEY MINT.... NOW TURN ME LOOSE!
I THINK I'LL WAIT 'TIL I GIT DE MONEY MINT FUST!
WELL, SUH, BRER RABBIT AIN'T SO SHO' NOW WHEDDER DIS MONEY MINT IS GOIN' TO PAY

Walt Disney Presents..
"UNCLE REMUS".
and his tales of BRER RABBIT
Based on the stories by JOEL CHANDLER HARRIS
RABBIT LOOSE IF HE TOLD HIM WHERE HIS MONEY MINT WAS AT... BUT NOW HE AIN'T SO SURE!
BUT IT'S DE TRUTH, BRER FOX... WHEN DEM HIND WHEELS KETCH UP WID DE FRONT WHEELS, DE GOLD FLIES OUT BY DE HATFUL!
BUT HOW DO I KNOW IT WORKS?
HOW DOES YOU KNO' SUGAR IS SWEET... 'LESS YOU TASTES IT?
DAR COMES A WAGON NOW!
BETTER GIT YO'SELF A MONEY MINT, BRER FOX!
DAR'S OUR CHANCE, BRER FOX ...UNTIE ME QUICK AN' LET'S ME AN' YOU GIT RICH!
UNTIE YOU? DAT'S JES' WHAT I AIN'T GOIN' TO DO!
IF DAR'S ANY MONEY TO BE GOT, DEN I'M GOIN' TO DO DE GITTIN'!
YOU STAYS RIGHT HERE! AN' IF DAR AIN'T NO MONEY IN DAT MINT... DEN I'M COMIN' RIGHT BACK AN' MINCE YOU!
BUT YOU'LL NEED ME TO HELP CARRY DE MONEY!
I AIN'T NEEDED NOBODY YET TO HELP ME CARRY MONEY!
3-10
YESSUH.. DEM BIG WHEELS IS BOUND TO KETCH UP WID DEM LITTLE WHEELS PRETTY SOON NOW!
NOW I IS IN A MESS!
PO' BRER RABBIT... HE CAN'T GIT LOOSE AN' HE KNOWS WHAT BRER FOX WILL DO WHEN HE COMES BACK WIDOUT DE MONEY MINT!
CONTINUED.

Walt Disney
Presents..
"UNCLE REMUS"
and his tales of BRER RABBIT
Based on the stories by JOEL CHANDLER HARRIS
BRER FOX DONE GONE OFF, FOLLOWIN' DE WAGON TO GIT BRER RABBIT'S MONEY MINT ...BUT IF HE DON'T GIT IT (WHICH HE AIN'T) HE'S COMIN' BACK TO GIT BRER RABBIT!
WHEN DE BIG WHEELS KETCH UP WID DE LITTLE ONES...DE GOLD FLIES OUT BY DE HATFUL!
AIN'T DAT BRER RABBIT TIED TO DAT TREE?
IT LOOKS LIKE I AIN'T EVER GOIN' TO GIT LOOSE!
WHAT IN DE WORL' ARE YOU DOIN' TIED UP?
OH...WHY...ER...I MUSTA FELL ASLEEP AN' SOME OF DE BOYS PLAYED A PRANK ON ME!
DEM POSSUM BOYS IS ALWAYS UP TO SOME KIND OF TRICKS!
BEND OVER DAR AN' I'LL CUT YOU LOOSE!
BRER TARRYPIN, YOU IS A REAL FRIEND!
WHAT DOES YOU HEAR FROM BRER FOX?
OH...DE LAST I HEARD FROM HIM, HE WUZ ON HIS WAY TO MISSISSLIPPY!
BRER FOX AIN'T VERY SMART... IS HE?
OH, HE'S SMART ALL RIGHT ...BUT HE AIN'T SMART IN DE RIGHT PLACE AT DE RIGHT TIME!
THANK YOU, BRER TARRYPIN, THANK YOU...WHEN I DIES, DOES YOU KNO' WHAT I'M GOIN' TO DO FER YOU?..
...I'M GOIN' TO LEAVE YOU MY MONEY MINT!
BRER RABBIT, YOU IS A GEN'ROUS MAN!
A GOOD FRIEND IS FORTUNE ENUF!

Walt Disney's Donald Duck in "Race to the South Seas!"
LISTEN, COUSIN GLADSTONE GANDER, MY SIDE OF THE FAMILY HAS ALWAYS BEEN BETTER THAN YOUR SIDE!
HOW WOULD I KNOW? US GANDERS HAVE NEVER SUNK LOW ENOUGH TO ASSOCIATE WITH YOU DUCKS!
W MOC 41-01
AMONG US DUCKS ARE GREAT LAWYERS, STATESMEN, DOCTORS —
PHOOEY! MERE TOILERS! US GANDERS HAVE NEVER WORKED!
AND MY UNCLE ON MY MOTHER'S SIDE IS SCROOGE McDUCK, THE RICHEST MAN IN THE WORLD!
SO WHAT?
SCROOGE McDUCK IS MY MOTHER'S BROTHER'S BROTHER-IN-LAW, AND I'M GOING TO GET A BIG CUT OF HIS FORTUNE, TOO!
I'M HIS FAVORITE RELATIVE! HE WOULDN'T GIVE YOU THE MOTHS OUT OF HIS BILLFOLD!
IS THAT SO?
SAY, AREN'T YOU GLADSTONE GANDER, SON OF SCROOGE McDUCK'S SISTER-IN-LAW?
SURE! WHO'S SUING ME NOW?
I HAVE GOOD NEWS FOR YOU! MR. McDUCK HAS GIVEN YOU A WONDERFUL PRESENT!
ULP!
!

THAT SAILBOAT IS YOURS, WITH MR. McDUCK'S REGARDS!
I-I CAN'T BELIEVE IT!
YOU MEAN HE-HE ACTUALLY GAVE ME THAT BOAT!
IT MUST BE A GAG! WHO ARE YOU, ANYWAY, MISTER?
?
SYLVESTER SHYSTER, MR. McDUCK'S PERSONAL LAWYER! I'LL READ HIS STATEMENT ABOUT THE GIFT!
"WHEREAS THE SAID GLADSTONE GANDER IS SO FULL OF WIND HE CAN SAIL A BOAT ON A STILL DAY, I AM PRESENTING HIM THIS TWENTY-FOOT SAILING CRAFT!
"MY REASON FOR MAKING THIS GIFT IS THAT UNDER CODE 6-A-77 OF THE TAX LAWS I CAN SAVE $ 3, 876, 943. 85 IN INCOME TAXES! (SIGNED) SCROOGE McDUCK."
NOT VERY FLATTERING, BUT HE GAVE ME THE BOAT! WHAT WAS IT YOU SAID ABOUT YOU BEING HIS FAVORITE RELATIVE?
GRRR!
I'VE BEEN INSULTED! I'LL NEVER SPEAK TO UNCLE SCROOGE AGAIN- NEVER!
POOR
UNCA'
DONALD!
WAIT A MINUTE, YOUNG FELLOW! IF YOU'RE DONALD DUCK, I HAVE GOOD NEWS FOR YOU, TOO, FROM MR. McDUCK!

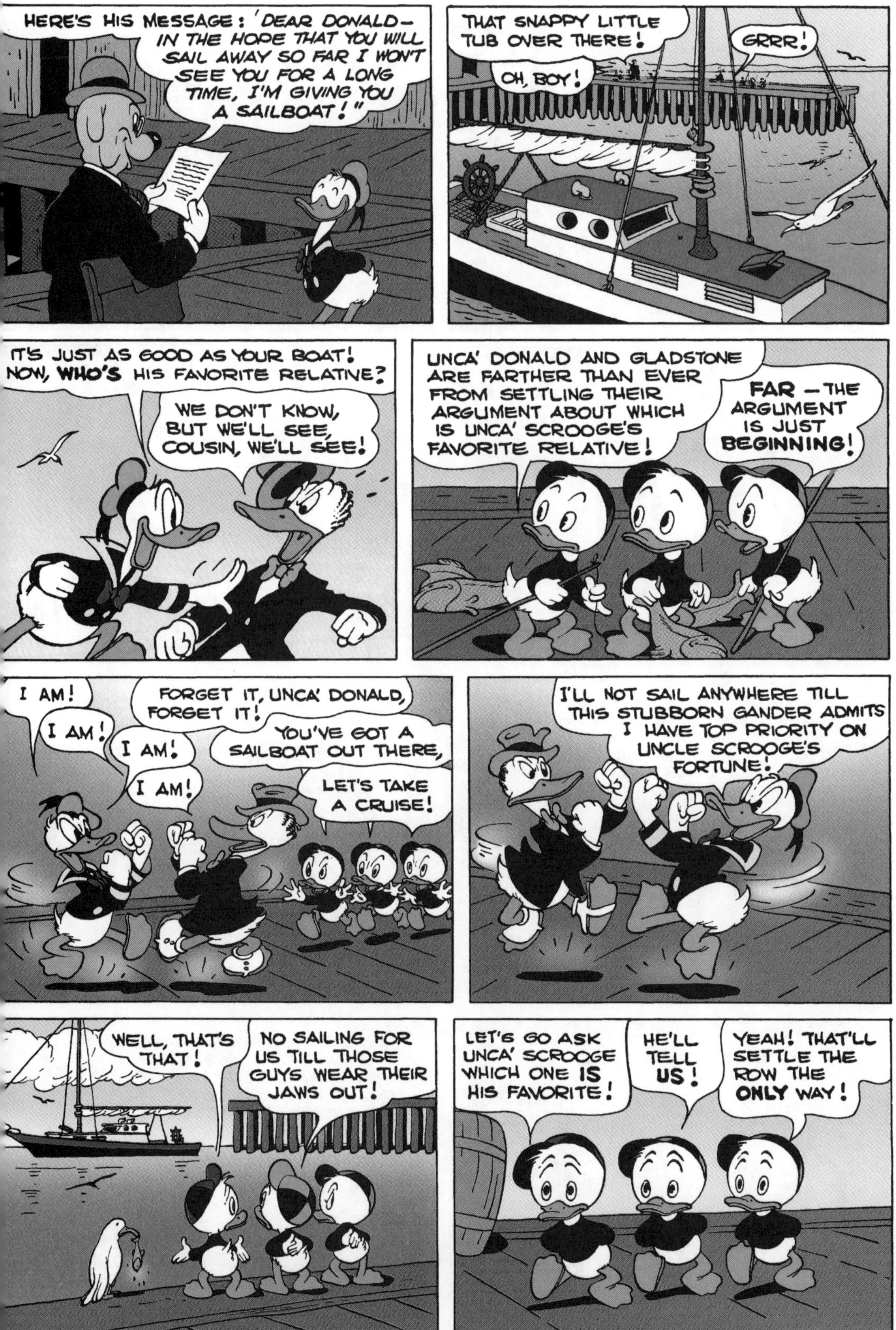
HERE'S HIS MESSAGE: 'DEAR DONALD— IN THE HOPE THAT YOU WILL SAIL AWAY SO FAR I WON'T SEE YOU FOR A LONG TIME, I'M GIVING YOU A SAILBOAT!'"
THAT SNAPPY LITTLE TUB OVER THERE!
OH, BOY!
GRRR!
IT'S JUST AS GOOD AS YOUR BOAT! NOW, WHO'S HIS FAVORITE RELATIVE?
WE DON'T KNOW, BUT WE'LL SEE, COUSIN, WE'LL SEE!
UNCA' DONALD AND GLADSTONE ARE FARTHER THAN EVER FROM SETTLING THEIR ARGUMENT ABOUT WHICH IS UNCA' SCROOGE'S FAVORITE RELATIVE!
FAR—THE ARGUMENT IS JUST BEGINNING!
I AM!
I AM!
I AM!
I AM!
FORGET IT, UNCA' DONALD, FORGET IT!
YOU'VE GOT A SAILBOAT OUT THERE,
LET'S TAKE A CRUISE!
I'LL NOT SAIL ANYWHERE TILL THIS STUBBORN GANDER ADMITS I HAVE TOP PRIORITY ON UNCLE SCROOGE'S FORTUNE!
WELL, THAT'S THAT!
NO SAILING FOR US TILL THOSE GUYS WEAR THEIR JAWS OUT!
LET'S GO ASK UNCA' SCROOGE WHICH ONE IS HIS FAVORITE!
HE'LL TELL US!
YEAH! THAT'LL SETTLE THE ROW THE ONLY WAY!

WE WANT TO SEE UNCA' SCROOGE RIGHT AWAY!
CAN'T DO, BOYS! HE'S OUT OF TOWN!
$CROOGE McDUCK VERY PRIVATE
HE FLEW TO AUSTRALIA THIS MORNING TO COUNT HIS EIGHT BILLION SHEEP! WON'T BE HOME UNTIL TOMORROW!
IT'S AWFULLY IMPORTANT! WE'LL COME BACK AS SOON AS HE RETURNS!
SECRETARY
OF ALL THE KINDS OF LUCK WE HAVE ONLY ONE KIND!
YEAH, BAD!
BAD AND BADDER!
McDUCK BUILDING BUILT WITH YOUR MONEY
HEY! THE HEADLINES ON THAT PAPER! LOOK AT THOSE HEADLINES!
FIVE MINUTES LATER!
UNCA' DONALD! UNCA' DONALD! THIS PAPER SAYS UNCA' SCROOGE IS LOST IN A STORM IN THE SOUTH SEAS!
UNCLE SCROOGE? DID YOU SAY UNCLE SCROOGE?
LET ME SEE THAT PAPER!
"WORLD'S RICHEST MAN FEARED CASTAWAY ON SOME LONELY ISLAND! WRECKAGE OF HIS PALATIAL FLYING BOAT FOUND ON UNCHARTED REEF!
DUCKBURG DRIBBLE

"NAVY SEARCH PARTIES RETURN EMPTY-HANDED! NEED SMALL BOATS TO COMB REMOTE LAGOONS AND SHALLOWS OF WRECK AREA!"
SALE 99% OFF
WHAT ARE YOU NOSING IN HERE ABOUT? GO BUY YOUR OWN PAPER!
DUCKBURG DRIBBLE
SIMMER DOWN, COUSIN, OL' PAL! I WAS JUST GETTIN' A BRIGHT IDEA!
I DON'T TRUST YOUR IDEAS!
I WAS THINKING THAT IF MY DEAR OLD RELATIVE IS A CASTAWAY ON A LONELY ISLAND, HE'S GOING TO BE MIGHTY GRATEFUL TO WHOEVER RESCUES HIM!
AND, BEING AS I HAVE A SMALL BOAT, I CAN SAIL RIGHT INTO THOSE LAGOONS AND RESCUE HIM!
YOU WILL IF THE KIDS AND I DON'T RESCUE HIM FIRST!
OH? SO IT'S GOING TO BE A RACE, HUH?
YES! AND IF YOU WANT TO GET TOUGH ABOUT IT– BLAH! BLAH!
I'LL GO SEE ABOUT WATER FOR THE VOYAGE!
I'LL GO SEE ABOUT EATS, AND OIL FOR THE GALLEY!
I'LL GO SEE ABOUT CHARTS AND WEATHER MAPS!

PREPARING FOR A LONG VOYAGE TAKES TIME AND MONEY! THE DUCKS GO ALL-OUT TO MAKE THEIR LITTLE BOAT READY FOR ITS BATTLE WITH THE STORMY SEAS!
HAVE WE GOT SALT BUTTER FOR OUR BREAD?
NO!
YES! HAVE WE GOT BREAD?
LOOK AT GLADSTONE! HE DOES NOTHING BUT SAIL AROUND THE BAY!
AND TALK BIG ABOUT RESCUING UNCA' SCROOGE!
SWELL! LET THE BIG SHOW-OFF HAVE HIS FUN! WE'LL BE HALFWAY TO THE SOUTH SEAS BEFORE HE GETS STARTED!
I WOULDN'T BE TOO SURE OF THAT! GLADSTONE WAS BORN LUCKY! HE DOESN'T HAVE TO LOAD HIS BOAT! SANTA CLAUS WILL DO THAT!
THAT EVENING!
WELL, EVERYTHING IS LOADED AND SHIPSHAPE! WE'LL ANCHOR IN OPEN WATER, SO AS TO BE READY TO SAIL WITH THE FIRST PUFF OF WIND!
FROM NOW ON I'M CAPTAIN, AND YOU'LL CALL ME 'SIR'!
AYE,
AYE,
SIR!
WE'RE READY TO SAIL, AND THERE'S GLADSTONE STILL TALKING BIG TO NEWSPAPER REPORTERS!
I DON'T LIKE IT!
LATER!
WHAT'S MAKING ALL THAT NOISE?
THE RACKET IS OVER BY THE DOCK!

IT'S A BUNCH OF MEN LOADING SUPPLIES INTO GLADSTONE'S BOAT!
AND GLADSTONE IS LOAFING ON TOP OF THE CABIN, PLAYING BIG SHOT AND TAKING IT EASY!
LISTEN! OUR RADIO—
GLADSTONE GANDER, COURAGEOUS NEPHEW-IN-LAW OF LOST TRILLIONAIRE SCROOGE McDUCK, SAILS AT DAWN FOR THE SOUTH SEAS TO RESCUE HIS RICH RELATIVE!
NOT A WORD ABOUT **US**!
TOUCHED BY GANDER'S HEROISM, LOCAL SHIP CHANDLERS ARE LOADING HIS TINY CRAFT WITH A COMPLETE STOCK OF **FREE** PROVISIONS!
UNCA' DONALD, YOU'RE TURNING **PURPLE**!
I KNEW IT! I KNEW IT! THAT GANDER GETS **EVERY** BREAK! HE'LL BEAT US TO UNCLE SCROOGE! WE HAVEN'T A CHANCE!
SIMMER DOWN, UNCA' DONALD! THE ISLANDS ARE A LONG WAY OFF!
ANYTHING CAN HAPPEN!
ANYTHING CAN HAPPEN TO **US**, BUT ONLY **GOOD** THINGS CAN HAPPEN TO **HIM**!

THE BREEZE, THE FOG, AND THE SUN ALL RISE AT THE SAME TIME!
THE SAIL'S FILLING, SIR!
HOIST THE ANCHOR! WE'RE OFF!
DOWN THE HARBOR TO THE BREAKWATER! THEN OUT TO THE OPEN SEA!
QUACK
GLADSTONE'S BOAT IS STILL ANCHORED BY THE DOCK!
HE MUST BE SLEEPING LATE—AS USUAL!
I HOPE HE SLEEPS TILL NOON OF NEXT YEAR!
LET'S SEE NOW! IF I WANT TO GO LEFT, I TURN THE WHEEL TO THE RIGHT—OR DO I?
LOOKOUT, UNCA' DONALD! YOU'RE GOING TO HIT A BUOY!
LUFF THE JIBSAIL! BELAY THE MARLINSPIKES! I'M PORTING THE FOC'SILL TO STARBOARD!
NO! NO, UNCA' DONALD! LOOK OUT—THE BOOM!
SWISH!
WHAT'S WRONG WITH THIS CRAZY BOAT?
NOTHING! YOU JUST TURNED HE TOO SHARP ACROSS THE WIND!

FURL THE SPINNAKERS! CROSSJACK THE MIZZENSHROUDS!
WHAT KIND OF LINGO IS THAT?
YOUR ORDERS DON'T MAKE SENSE, UNCA' DONALD!
RUN UP THE FOREGALLANT MAINBRACE—AND CALL ME SIR!
YOU'RE DRIFTING ONTO A SANDBAR, SIR!
CRUNCH!
LOOKS LIKE WE'RE STUCK HERE FOR AWHILE!
WE'LL FLOAT OFF AT HIGH TIDE! SHUT UP!
WELL, WELL, CAPTAIN DUCK RUNS HIS SHIP AGROUND! I'LL SEND A TUG BACK FROM TAHITI TO PULL YOU OFF!
GLADSTONE!
I TOLD YOU KIDS THAT GUY WOULD BEAT US! I TOLD YOU SO!
DEWEY, GIVE ME A HAND IN THE CABIN FOR A MINUTE!
HELP ME GET THAT BOOK FROM UNDER THOSE CHARTS!
OH, BOY! JUST WHAT THE CAPTAIN NEEDS!
HOW TO SAIL A BOAT

THE TIDES AND THE WINDS AND A GOOD BOOK WORK WONDERS FOR THE FOUR DUCKS! BY DAWN OF ANOTHER DAY THEY ARE FAR OUT AT SEA!
COMPASS READING WEST BY SOUTHWEST!
WIND TEN KNOTS!
ALL SAILS TIGHT AS DRUMHEADS!
IF GLADSTONE COULD SEE US CUTTING WATER LIKE THIS, HE'D SHAKE IN HIS SPATS!
BOAT, AHOY! I SEE A SAIL! I MEAN A BOAT WITH SAILS FURLED!
IT'S GLADSTONE!
HE'S STOPPED TO FISH!
WET A LINE, COUSIN THEY'RE BITING FINE!
I DON'T GO FISHING IN THE MIDDLE OF A RACE!
POUR ON MORE SAIL, BOYS!
I COULD FISH HERE FOR A WEEK AND STILL BEAT YOU TO UNCLE SCROOGE'S ISLAND!
YIPPEE! I'VE HOOKED A BIG ONE!
TWANG!
AND LOOK! HE'S GOING WEST BY SOUTHWEST AT FIFTY KNOTS AN HOUR!
SEE, KIDS? SEE WHAT I MEAN?

THE WIND IS RISING, UNCA' DONALD— SIR!
AND THAT OVERCAST LOOKS BAD! WE'RE IN FOR A BLOW!
CLOSE HAUL THE SAILS, BOYS! AND LASH DOWN THE POTS AND PANS! ROUGH SEAS AHEAD!
IT'S A TYPHOON!
ROAR
CRACK
THERE GOES OUR MAST!
CRACK!
BAM!
AND THERE GOES OUR RUDDER AND STEERING POST!
AND THERE GOES OUR CHANCE TO WIN THE RACE TO UNCLE SCROOGE!
I WOULDN'T BE TOO SURE OF THAT, UNCA' DONALD! GLADSTONE IS SITTING OVER HERE, AND HIS BOAT IS JUST AS BUNGED UP AS OURS!

THE STORM PASSES, AND CALM, HOT AND DEADLY, SETTLES OVER THE BROAD OCEAN!
DIG OUT THE OARS, BOYS! WE'LL HAVE TO PADDLE! CAN'T SIT HERE AND EAT UP OUR GROCERIES!
AHOY, GLADSTONE! ARE YOU GOING TO SIT THERE AND DRY UP? START ROWING!
ME...ROW?
I'VE NEVER STOOPED TO MENIAL LABOR! LEAVE ME ALONE! SOMEBODY WILL COME ALONG AND GIVE ME A LIFT!
A WHALE IS COMING UP ASTERN, UNCA' DONALD — I MEAN, SIR!
WATCH HIM DIVE! WOW!
HE'S COMING UP UNDER GLADSTONE'S BOAT!
AND SWIMMING AWAY WITH IT ON HIS BACK!
TRAVELING WEST SOUTHWEST TOWARD TAHITI! SEE YOU IN THE FUNNY PAPERS, BOYS!

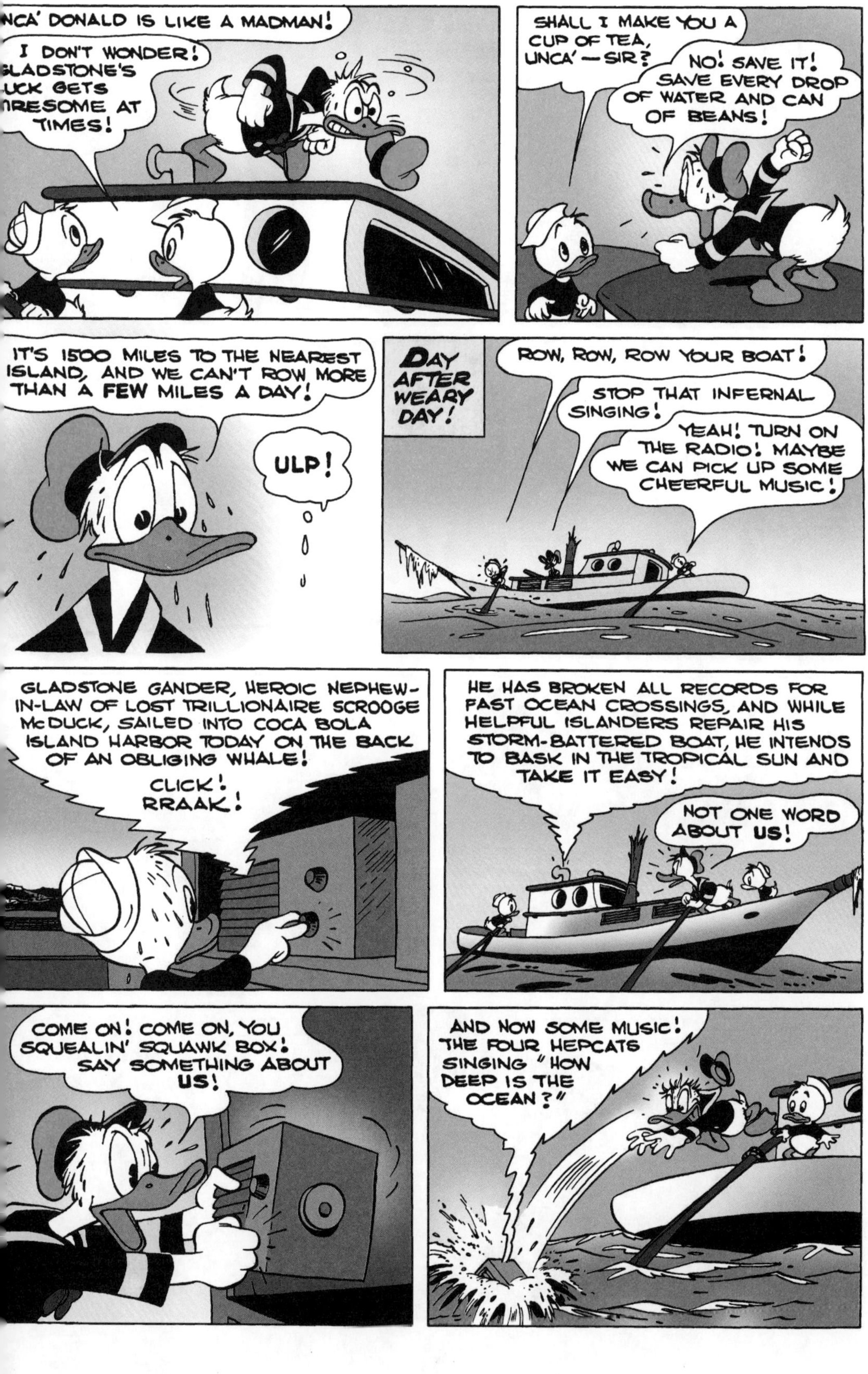

NCA' DONALD IS LIKE A MADMAN!
I DON'T WONDER! GLADSTONE'S LUCK GETS TIRESOME AT TIMES!
SHALL I MAKE YOU A CUP OF TEA, UNCA'—SIR?
NO! SAVE IT! SAVE EVERY DROP OF WATER AND CAN OF BEANS!
IT'S 1500 MILES TO THE NEAREST ISLAND, AND WE CAN'T ROW MORE THAN A FEW MILES A DAY!
ULP!
DAY AFTER WEARY DAY!
ROW, ROW, ROW YOUR BOAT!
STOP THAT INFERNAL SINGING!
YEAH! TURN ON THE RADIO! MAYBE WE CAN PICK UP SOME CHEERFUL MUSIC!
GLADSTONE GANDER, HEROIC NEPHEW-IN-LAW OF LOST TRILLIONAIRE SCROOGE McDUCK, SAILED INTO COCA BOLA ISLAND HARBOR TODAY ON THE BACK OF AN OBLIGING WHALE!
CLICK! RRAAK!
HE HAS BROKEN ALL RECORDS FOR FAST OCEAN CROSSINGS, AND WHILE HELPFUL ISLANDERS REPAIR HIS STORM-BATTERED BOAT, HE INTENDS TO BASK IN THE TROPICAL SUN AND TAKE IT EASY!
NOT ONE WORD ABOUT US!
COME ON! COME ON, YOU SQUEALIN' SQUAWK BOX! SAY SOMETHING ABOUT US!
AND NOW SOME MUSIC! THE FOUR HEPCATS SINGING "HOW DEEP IS THE OCEAN?"

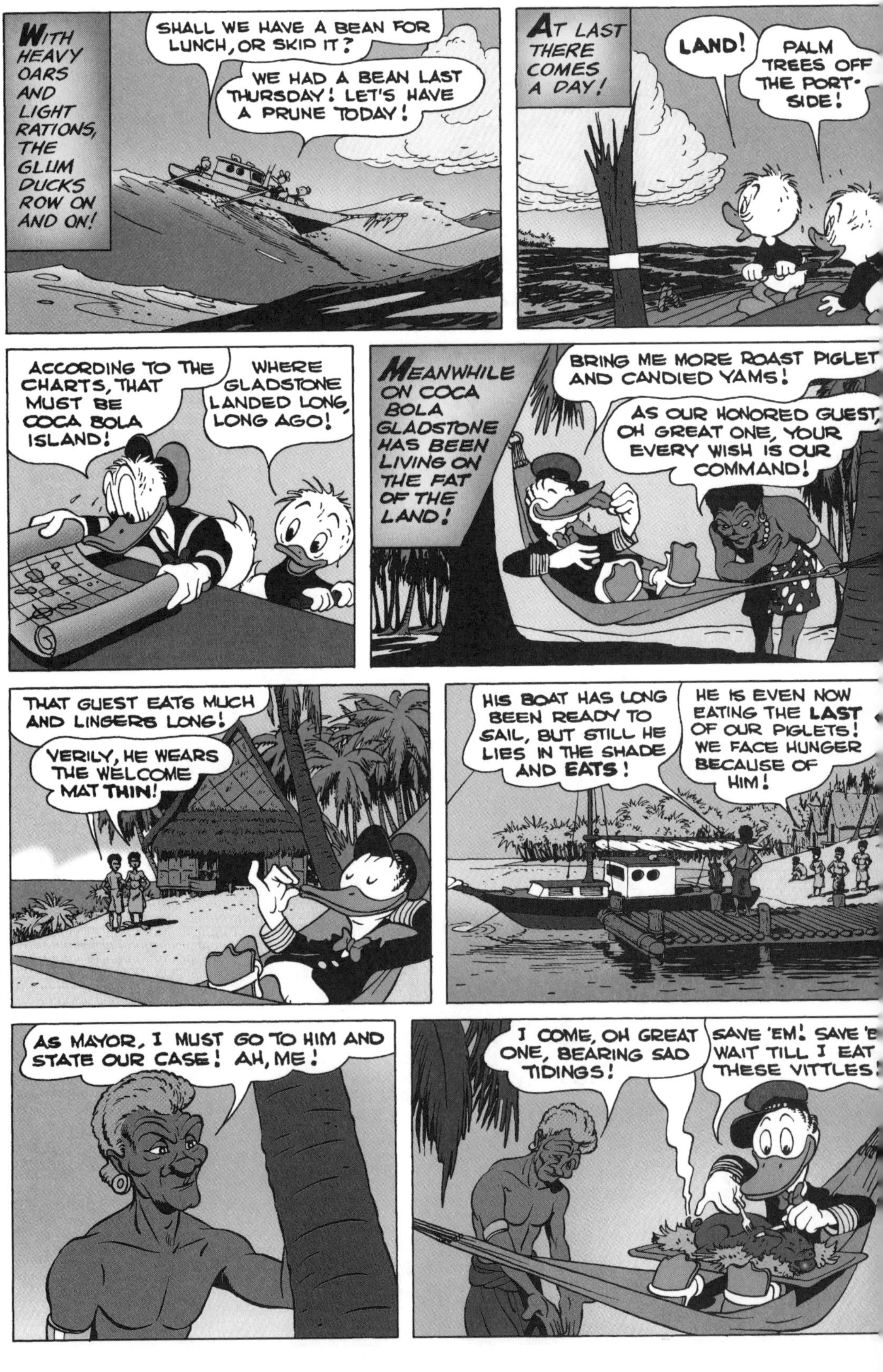
WITH HEAVY OARS AND LIGHT RATIONS, THE GLUM DUCKS ROW ON AND ON!
SHALL WE HAVE A BEAN FOR LUNCH, OR SKIP IT?
WE HAD A BEAN LAST THURSDAY! LET'S HAVE A PRUNE TODAY!
AT LAST THERE COMES A DAY!
LAND!
PALM TREES OFF THE PORT-SIDE!
ACCORDING TO THE CHARTS, THAT MUST BE COCA BOLA ISLAND!
WHERE GLADSTONE LANDED LONG, LONG AGO!
MEANWHILE ON COCA BOLA GLADSTONE HAS BEEN LIVING ON THE FAT OF THE LAND!
BRING ME MORE ROAST PIGLET AND CANDIED YAMS!
AS OUR HONORED GUEST, OH GREAT ONE, YOUR EVERY WISH IS OUR COMMAND!
THAT GUEST EATS MUCH AND LINGERS LONG!
VERILY, HE WEARS THE WELCOME MAT THIN!
HIS BOAT HAS LONG BEEN READY TO SAIL, BUT STILL HE LIES IN THE SHADE AND EATS!
HE IS EVEN NOW EATING THE LAST OF OUR PIGLETS! WE FACE HUNGER BECAUSE OF HIM!
AS MAYOR, I MUST GO TO HIM AND STATE OUR CASE! AH, ME!
I COME, OH GREAT ONE, BEARING SAD TIDINGS!
SAVE 'EM! SAVE 'E WAIT TILL I EAT THESE VITTLES!

THE VITTLES ARE THE SAD TIDINGS, OH HONORED ONE! THERE **ISN'T ANY MORE**!
WHAT?
NO MORE ROAST PIGLETS? NO MORE CANDIED YAMS AND GRAVIED SWEETBREADS?
YOU CAN SAY THAT AGAIN! OUR PANTRY IS EMPTY!
AND JUST WHEN I WAS BEGINNING TO LIKE THIS PLACE! WHAT ELSE DO YOU HAVE TO EAT?
COCONUTS!
I DON'T LIKE 'EM! HOW FAR IS IT TO THE NEXT ISLAND?
TWO DAYS GOOD WIND TO THE SOUTH!
OT BAD! GIVE ME EVERYTHING YOU HAVE LEFT IN YOUR KITCHENS, AND I'LL BE ON MY WAY!
OH, WHAT A RELIEF!
HE'S GONE!
HE ATE US INTO THE POORHOUSE! BUT HE **DID** TEACH US A LESSON!
YES! AFTER THIS, WHEN SHIPWRECKED MARINERS COME TO OUR ISLAND, WE'LL KNOW **HOW** TO TREAT 'EM!
AT THAT MOMENT!
COCA BOLA ISLAND!
FAMED FOR IT'S **GENEROUS** HOSPITALITY!
I ONLY HOPE THE NATIVES WON'T MAKE US EAT **TOO** MUCH!

UH, OH! SOMETHING'S WRONG! THESE GUYS DON'T LOOK AS IF THEY LIKE US!
YOU CAN SAY THAT AGAIN, MISTER!
NEXT DAY!
WOW! WHAT A WELCOME THEY GAVE US!
EVERYTHING WE GOT WE PAID FOR!
AND SUCH PRICES!
WELL, OUR NEW MAST AND SAILS WERE COSTLY, BUT THEY'LL TAKE US WHERE WE WANT TO GO!
HAVE ANOTHER TWO-DOLLAR COCONUT!
UGH!
WHAT'S THE PROGRAM NOW, UNCA-SIR?
MORE SAILING! ANOTHER OUTFITTING AT TAHITI, THEN SOUTH TO WHERE UNCLE SCROOGE CRACKE UP!
THE ARCHIPELAGO OF YAPAYAPAYAP! BROODING, MYSTERIOUS EXPANSE OF SEA-SWEPT CORAL ATOLLS, ONE OF EARTH'S LEAST-KNOWN PLACES, HERE UNCLE SCROOGE McDUCK DISAPPEARED! HE WOULD!
THERE'S THE REEF WHERE THEY FOUND UNCLE SCROOGE'S PLANE!
HE COULD PADDLE TO ANY OF THESE ISLANDS WITH A LIFE RAFT!
TAKE THE TILLER, LOUIE, AND SAIL ALONG SLOW! I WANT TO SCAN THESE COCONUT DUNES WITH MY SPYGLASS!

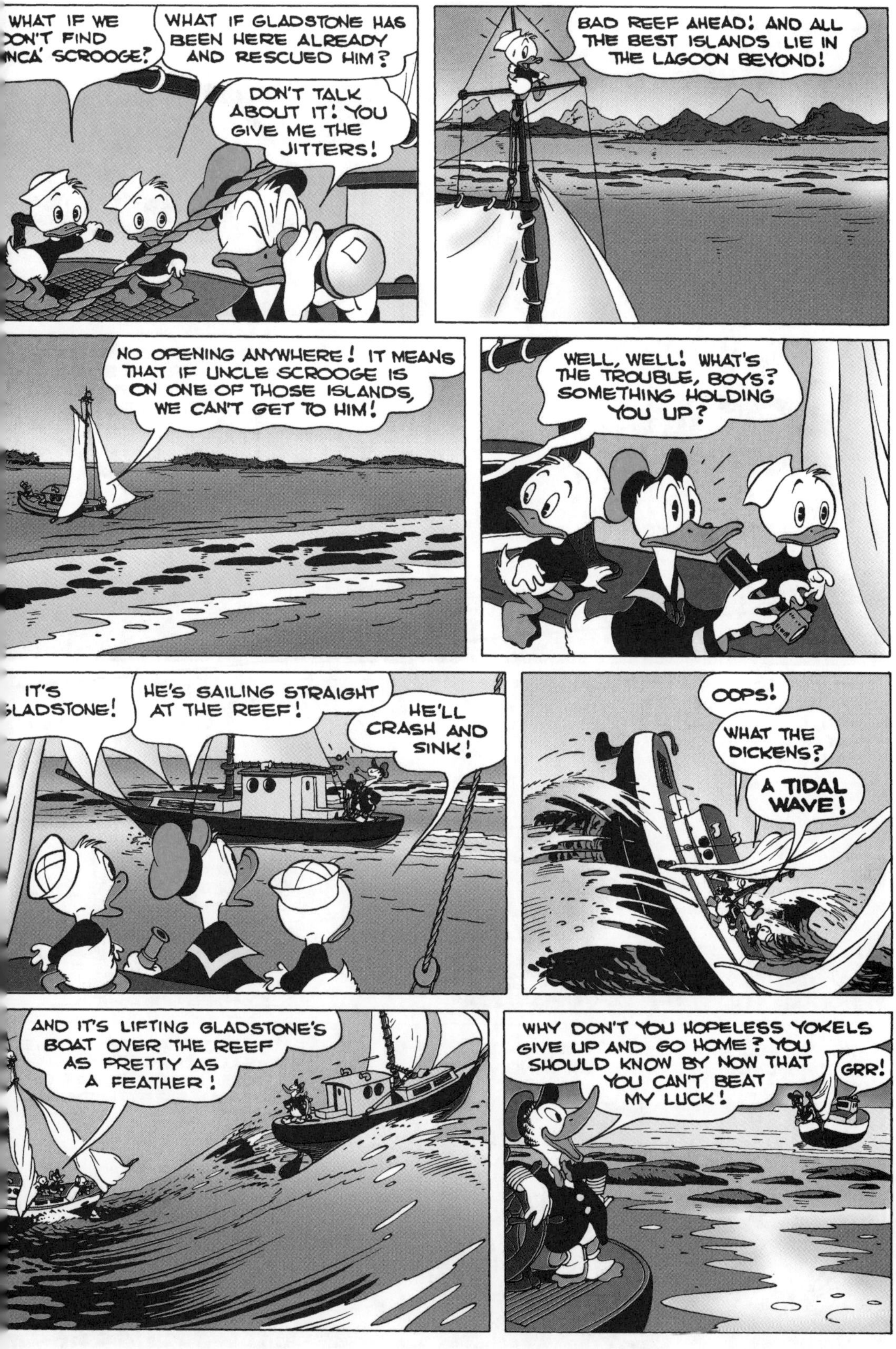
WHAT IF WE
DON'T FIND
UNCA' SCROOGE?
WHAT IF GLADSTONE HAS BEEN HERE ALREADY AND RESCUED HIM?
DON'T TALK ABOUT IT! YOU GIVE ME THE JITTERS!
BAD REEF AHEAD! AND ALL THE BEST ISLANDS LIE IN THE LAGOON BEYOND!
NO OPENING ANYWHERE! IT MEANS THAT IF UNCLE SCROOGE IS ON ONE OF THOSE ISLANDS, WE CAN'T GET TO HIM!
WELL, WELL! WHAT'S THE TROUBLE, BOYS? SOMETHING HOLDING YOU UP?
IT'S
GLADSTONE!
HE'S SAILING STRAIGHT AT THE REEF!
HE'LL CRASH AND SINK!
OOPS!
WHAT THE DICKENS?
A TIDAL WAVE!
AND IT'S LIFTING GLADSTONE'S BOAT OVER THE REEF AS PRETTY AS A FEATHER!
WHY DON'T YOU HOPELESS YOKELS GIVE UP AND GO HOME? YOU SHOULD KNOW BY NOW THAT YOU CAN'T BEAT MY LUCK!
GRR!

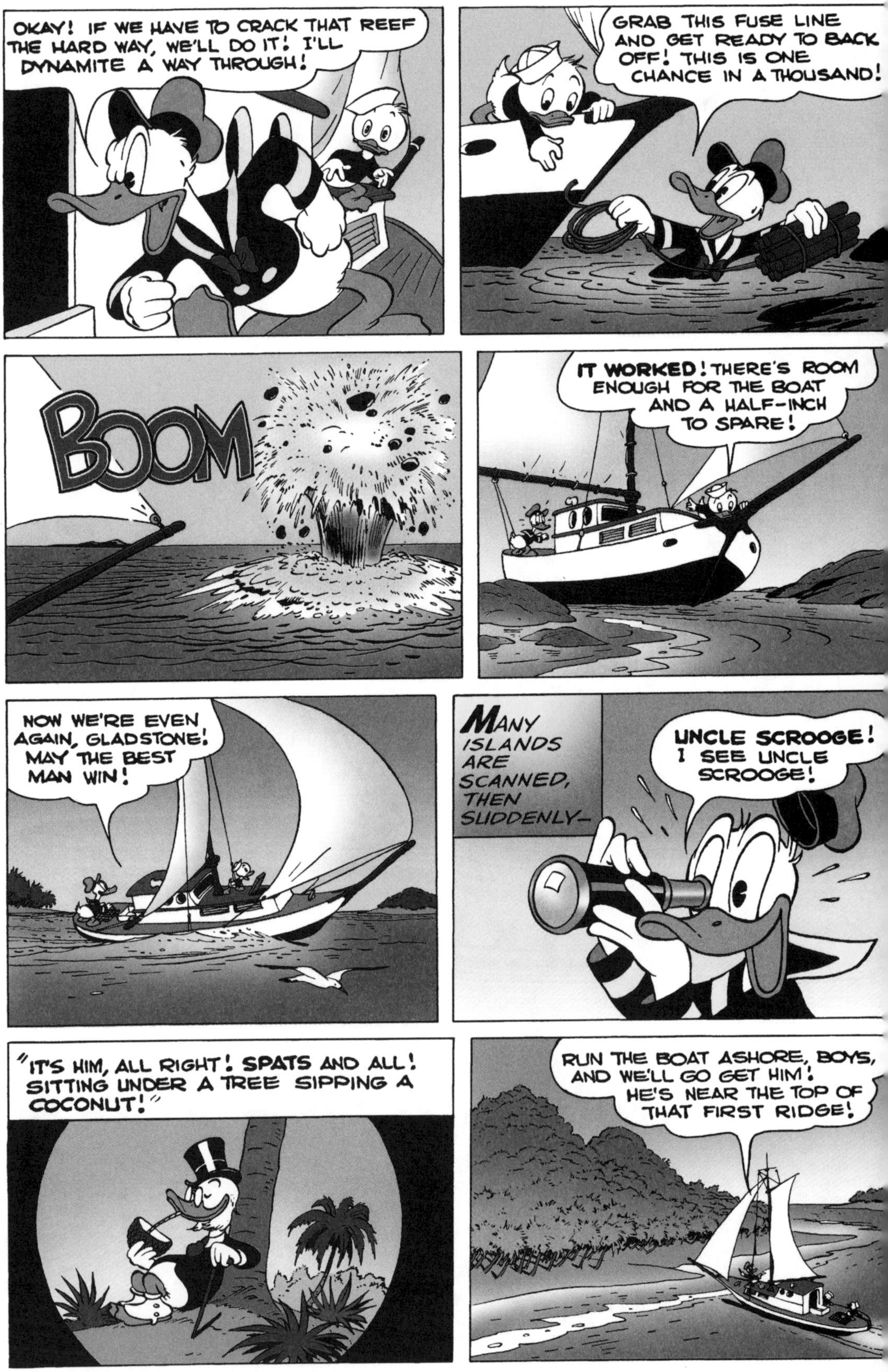
OKAY! IF WE HAVE TO CRACK THAT REEF THE HARD WAY, WE'LL DO IT! I'LL DYNAMITE A WAY THROUGH!
GRAB THIS FUSE LINE AND GET READY TO BACK OFF! THIS IS ONE CHANCE IN A THOUSAND!
BOOM
IT WORKED! THERE'S ROOM ENOUGH FOR THE BOAT AND A HALF-INCH TO SPARE!
NOW WE'RE EVEN AGAIN, GLADSTONE! MAY THE BEST MAN WIN!
MANY ISLANDS ARE SCANNED, THEN SUDDENLY—
UNCLE SCROOGE! I SEE UNCLE SCROOGE!
"IT'S HIM, ALL RIGHT! SPATS AND ALL! SITTING UNDER A TREE SIPPING A COCONUT!"
RUN THE BOAT ASHORE, BOYS, AND WE'LL GO GET HIM! HE'S NEAR THE TOP OF THAT FIRST RIDGE!

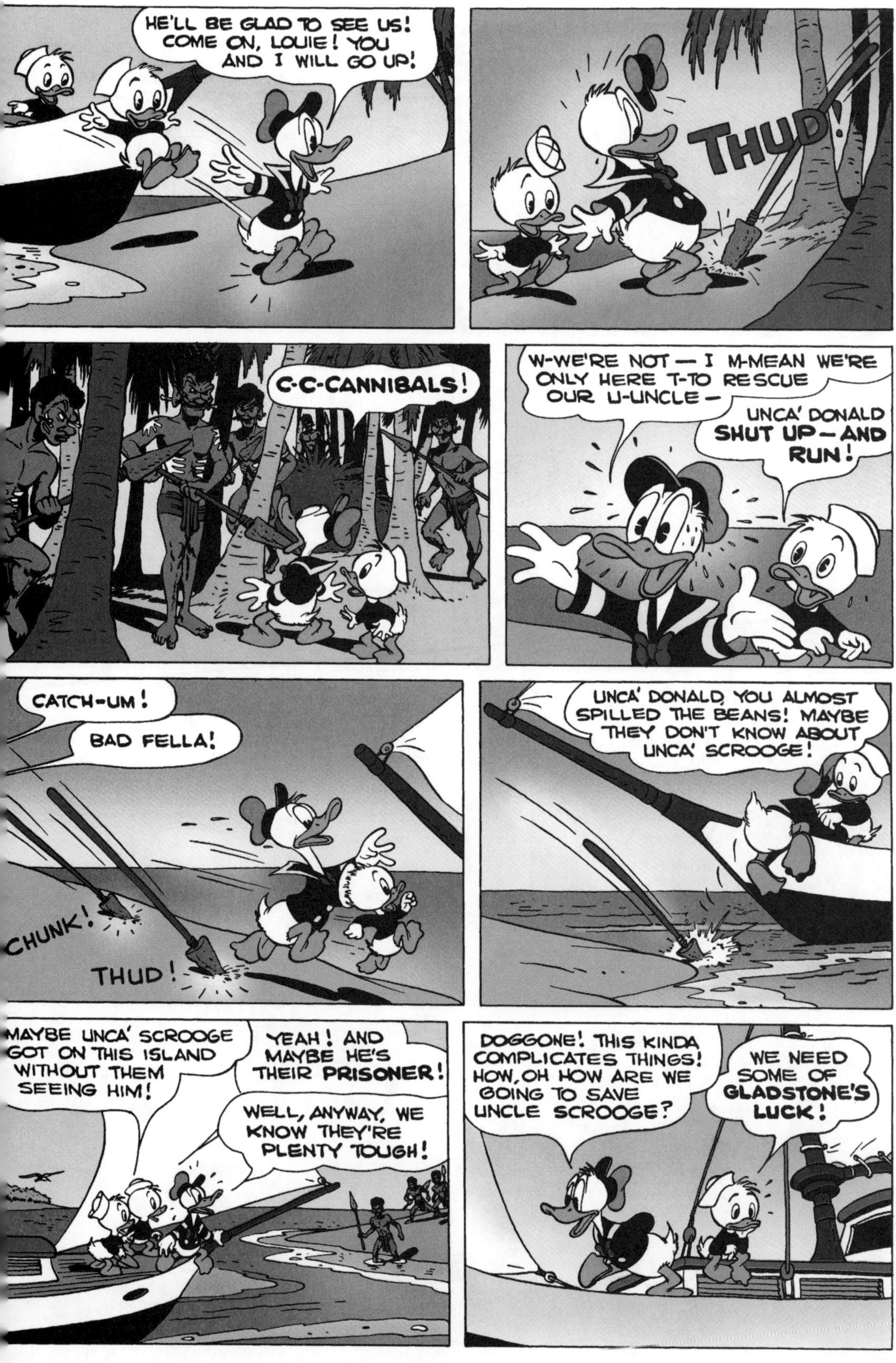
HE'LL BE GLAD TO SEE US! COME ON, LOUIE! YOU AND I WILL GO UP!
THUD!
C-C-CANNIBALS!
W-WE'RE NOT — I M-MEAN WE'RE ONLY HERE T-TO RESCUE OUR U-UNCLE —
UNCA' DONALD SHUT UP — AND RUN!
CATCH-UM!
BAD FELLA!
CHUNK!
THUD!
UNCA' DONALD, YOU ALMOST SPILLED THE BEANS! MAYBE THEY DON'T KNOW ABOUT UNCA' SCROOGE!
MAYBE UNCA' SCROOGE GOT ON THIS ISLAND WITHOUT THEM SEEING HIM!
YEAH! AND MAYBE HE'S THEIR PRISONER!
WELL, ANYWAY, WE KNOW THEY'RE PLENTY TOUGH!
DOGGONE! THIS KINDA COMPLICATES THINGS! HOW, OH HOW ARE WE GOING TO SAVE UNCLE SCROOGE?
WE NEED SOME OF GLADSTONE'S LUCK!

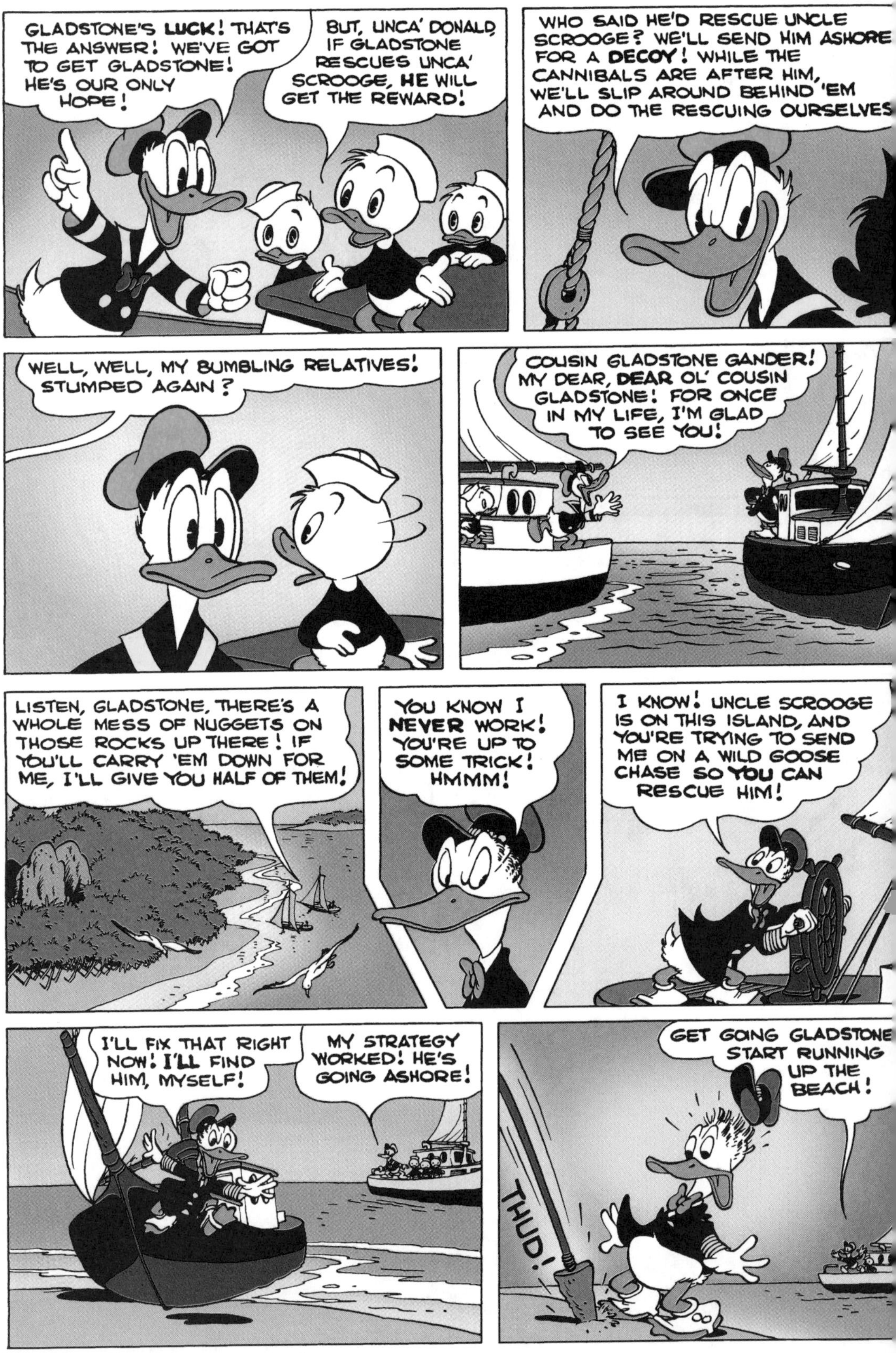

GLADSTONE'S LUCK! THAT'S THE ANSWER! WE'VE GOT TO GET GLADSTONE! HE'S OUR ONLY HOPE!
BUT, UNCA' DONALD, IF GLADSTONE RESCUES UNCA' SCROOGE, HE WILL GET THE REWARD!
WHO SAID HE'D RESCUE UNCLE SCROOGE? WE'LL SEND HIM ASHORE FOR A DECOY! WHILE THE CANNIBALS ARE AFTER HIM, WE'LL SLIP AROUND BEHIND 'EM AND DO THE RESCUING OURSELVES
WELL, WELL, MY BUMBLING RELATIVES! STUMPED AGAIN?
COUSIN GLADSTONE GANDER! MY DEAR, DEAR OL' COUSIN GLADSTONE! FOR ONCE IN MY LIFE, I'M GLAD TO SEE YOU!
LISTEN, GLADSTONE, THERE'S A WHOLE MESS OF NUGGETS ON THOSE ROCKS UP THERE! IF YOU'LL CARRY 'EM DOWN FOR ME, I'LL GIVE YOU HALF OF THEM!
YOU KNOW I NEVER WORK! YOU'RE UP TO SOME TRICK! HMMM!
I KNOW! UNCLE SCROOGE IS ON THIS ISLAND, AND YOU'RE TRYING TO SEND ME ON A WILD GOOSE CHASE SO YOU CAN RESCUE HIM!
I'LL FIX THAT RIGHT NOW! I'LL FIND HIM, MYSELF!
MY STRATEGY WORKED! HE'S GOING ASHORE!
GET GOING GLADSTONE START RUNNING UP THE BEACH!
THUD!

OLA EELA BOOKA MOOKA BOCKO MUCKA!
I'LL BE DOGGONED! MY SPATS FLOORED 'EM! THEY THINK I'M AN IDOL, OR SOMETHING!
THEY'RE CARRYING GLADSTONE AWAY IN A LITTER CHAIR—LIKE HE'S A KING!
CAN ANYTHING BEAT THAT GUY'S LUCK?
WE CAN! THEY'VE FORGOTTEN US! HERE WE GO TO GET UNCLE SCROOGE!
RIGHT UP HERE IS WHERE I SAW HIM!
WAIT, DEWEY! SOMETHING SCREWY HERE!
A BUSINESS OFFICE, WITH STENOGRAPHERS TELETYPES, AND EVERYTHING!
WHAT IN THUNDER IS THAT COMMOTION?
OH! IT'S ONE OF THE GUARDS!
WE BRING GREAT FELLA COME FROM SEA! HIM GOT WHITE FEET LIKE YOU FELLA, MASSA!
WHITE FEET! YOU MEAN SPATS?

THOSE CANNIBALS WEREN'T CANNIBALS!
THEY'RE UNCLE SCROOGE'S HIRED STOOGES!
GLADSTONE GANDER! YOU—YOU HERE!
I CAME TO RESCUE YOU, UNCLE SCROOGE!
I CAN BET YOU WERE GREATLY WORRIED ABOUT ME! DID DONALD COME, TOO?
NO, UNCLE SCROOGE! I'M SORRY ABOUT DONALD! HE JUST DIDN'T SEEM TO CARE!
I LIKE THAT! AND AS FOR YOU, GLADSTONE, I'M NOT YOUR UNCLE, AND I DON'T WANT TO BE RESCUED!
BUT—YOUR PLANE CRASHED—AND—
I HAD THAT PLANE CRASHED! I DID IT SO I COULD COME TO THIS PREPARED HIDE-OUT AND RUN MY BUSINESS WITHOUT SEEING ANY OF MY RELATIVES!
ULP!
AND NOW YOU FIND ME—EVEN HERE! JUST FOR THAT, I'M CUTTING YOU OUT OF MY WILL!
I'LL LEAVE MY FORTUNE TO DONALD DUCK, WHO WAS KIND ENOUGH TO KEEP HIS LONG-NOSED FACE OUT OF MY SIGHT! NOW GIT!
HOW'S OLD LUCKY GLADSTONE, TONIGHT?
YEAH! HOW DO YOU FEEL?
GRRR!
U.S.A.

WALT DISNEY presents
The LI'L BAD WOLF
YOU STAY OUTA MY CHICKEN YARD, OR I'LL BASH YOU, ZEKE WOLF!
OS 403-03
WHY DOESN'T YOUR POP TRY BUYING A CHICKEN SOMETIME ?
YES! IT WOULD SAVE HIM A LOT OF TROUBLE!
BUT IT'S AGAINST HIS PRINCIPLES! HE SAYS US WOLVES WERE MEANT TO STEAL CHICKENS... NOT BUY THEM!
POOR LI'L WOLF! HE TRIES SO HARD TO BE GOOD... AND HIS POP IS SUCH AN OLD MEANY!
THERE YOU ARE! I WAS WONDERIN' WHEN YOU WERE GONNA COME! FETCH TH' ARNICA!
OKAY, POP!
WHILLIKERS! WHEN ARE YOU GOING TO LEARN YOUR LESSON ?
OUCH! HEY! TAKE IT EASY... YOW!

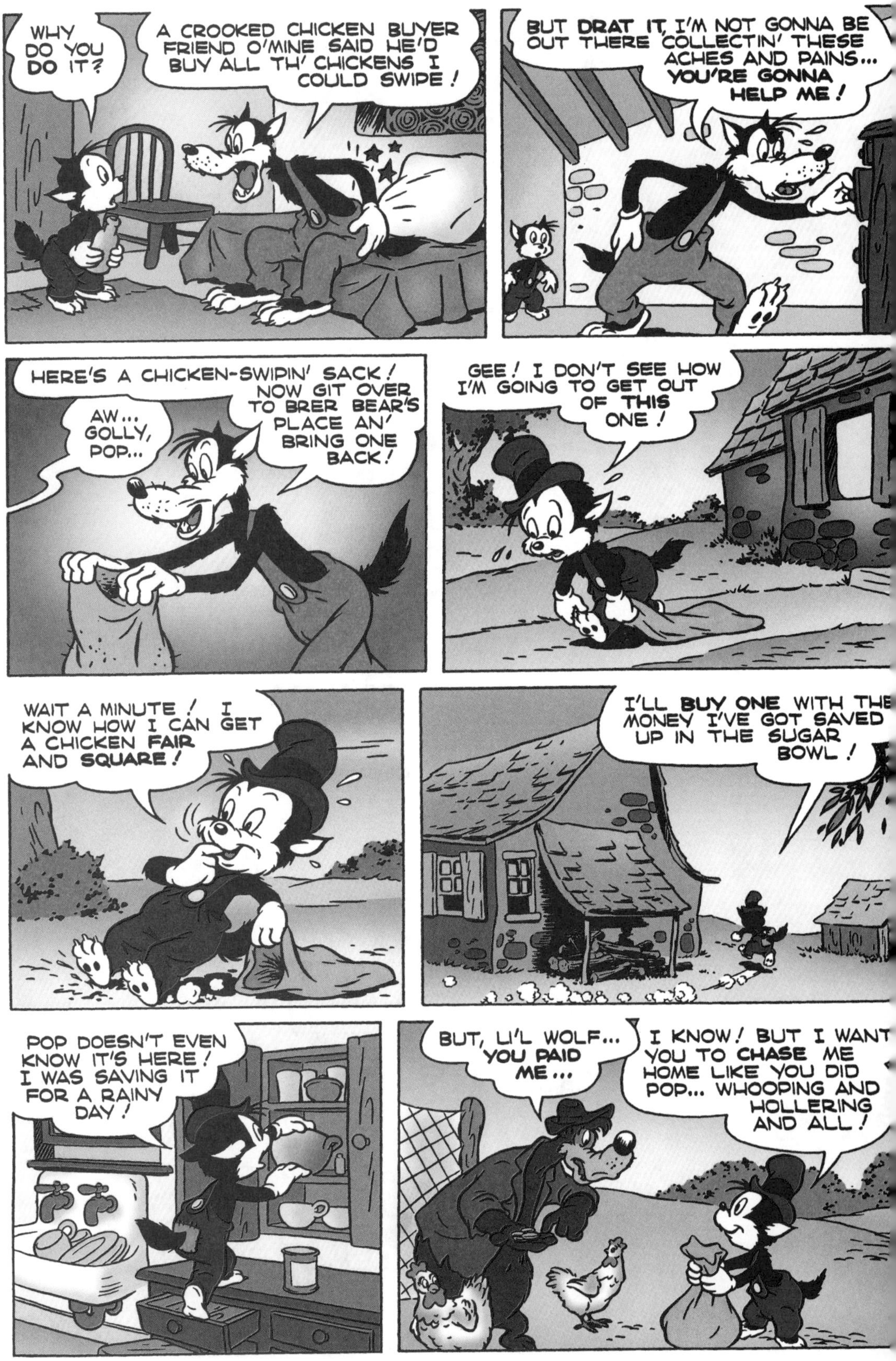
WHY DO YOU DO IT?
A CROOKED CHICKEN BUYER FRIEND O'MINE SAID HE'D BUY ALL TH' CHICKENS I COULD SWIPE!
BUT DRAT IT, I'M NOT GONNA BE OUT THERE COLLECTIN' THESE ACHES AND PAINS... YOU'RE GONNA HELP ME!
HERE'S A CHICKEN-SWIPIN' SACK! NOW GIT OVER TO BRER BEAR'S PLACE AN' BRING ONE BACK!
AW... GOLLY, POP...
GEE! I DON'T SEE HOW I'M GOING TO GET OUT OF THIS ONE!
WAIT A MINUTE! I KNOW HOW I CAN GET A CHICKEN FAIR AND SQUARE!
I'LL BUY ONE WITH THE MONEY I'VE GOT SAVED UP IN THE SUGAR BOWL!
POP DOESN'T EVEN KNOW IT'S HERE! I WAS SAVING IT FOR A RAINY DAY!
BUT, LI'L WOLF... YOU PAID ME...
I KNOW! BUT I WANT YOU TO CHASE ME HOME LIKE YOU DID POP... WHOOPING AND HOLLERING AND ALL!

POP SENT ME TO SWIPE A CHICKEN... AND HE'LL EXPECT IT TO LOOK GOOD!
AND SO...
WHOOP-DE-DO! WHOOP! WHOOP! WHOOP!
HOT DOGGIES! LI'L WOLF SNITCHED A CHICKEN! THAT'S GOOD... 'CAUSE TH' CHICKEN BUYER IS WAITIN' AT MY BACK DOOR!
SLAM
I'M PROUD OF YOU, SON! YOU'VE REALLY GOT TH' KNACK! YOU'LL GROW UP TO BE A REAL BAD WOLF AFTER ALL!
YES, INDEEDY! NOW TO DELIVER IT TO MY BUYER AT TH' BACK DOOR... TRA-LA-LA
POP'S SO HAPPY THINKING I REALLY SWIPED IT, THERE'S NO POINT IN SPOILING HIS FUN!
TUM DE DUM DUM TUM TUM TUM
THIS COULD TURN OUT TO BE A REAL GOOD THING!
I'D BETTER PUT THIS MONEY IN A SAFE SPOT... HM-M-M... TH' OL' SUGAR BOWL WOULD BE A PEACHY PLACE!
I'LL KEEP SENDIN' LI'L WOLF AFTER CHICKENS! HE MAY EVEN DEVELOP TH' HABIT HIMSELF!

B-BUT, POP...
YOU HEARD ME! TAKE THIS SACK AN' GET ANOTHER CHICKEN!
OH, DEAR! I'LL HAVE TO GO TO THE SUGAR BOWL AGAIN... BUT I DON'T THINK THERE'S ENOUGH FOR ANOTHER CHICKEN!
WHILLIKERS! THERE'S MORE HERE THAN I THOUGHT THERE WAS!
SO... LI'L WOLF MAKES ANOTHER TRIP TO BRER BEAR'S...
IN FACT... HE MAKES A LOT OF TRIPS!
MAN! THIS IS TH' UMPTEENTH CHICKEN YOU HAS BOUGHT TODAY! DO YOU STILL WANT ME TO CHASE YOU HOME?
YES, PLEASE BRER BEAR!
DIGGITY! HERE HE COMES... AN' BRER BEAR'S RAISIN' NED AGAIN!
HI-YA! WHOOP WHOOP! DE DOO!
SLAM
YOU'RE GETTIN' AWFUL GOO AT IT! BRER BEAR JUST CAN'T CATCH YOU!
I CAN'T FIGGER WHAT HE WANTS WITH ALL THEM CHICKENS... UNLESS HE'S FIXIN' TO HAVE A TERRIBLE WHOPPIN' BIG PICNIC!
THAT'S IT! I'LL BET HE'S GONNA HAVE ALL TH' CREATURES OVER FOR A CHICKEN FRY!

A CHICKEN FRY? WHO'S HAVING IT, BRER BEAR?
WH-WHY, AH... ZEKE WOLF! HE'S STOCKING UP WITH CHICKENS SOMETHIN' FIERCE!
SPREAD TH' WORD! TELL TH' CREATURES ALL ABOUT IT!
I WILL! I SURE WILL!
LATER...
BEFORE YOU GO OUT TO GET ANOTHER CHICKEN, SEE WHAT ALL THAT INFERNAL HUBBUB IS ABOUT!
YEA! HURRAH! 'RAY!
POP! IT'S A CROWD OF FOLKS WHO WANT TO KNOW WHEN THE CHICKEN DINNER STARTS!
WHAT!?
HMPH! I'LL SOON STOP THEM CRITTERS FROM HAVIN' THAT SILLY IDEA!
THIS WOULD BE YOUR BIG OPPORTUNITY, POP, TO SHOW THEM WHAT A FINE FELLOW YOU REALLY CAN BE!
ER... HUH?
WHY... SOMETHIN' LIKE THAT IS LIABLE TO RUIN MY REPUTATION AS A BIG BAD WOLF!
WELL... ER... OKAY! GO TELL THE CRITTERS WE'LL HAVE A BIG CHICKEN FRY!
SWELL, POP! THEY'LL BE TICKLED PINK!

HEE, HEE! IT WON'T COST ME NOTHIN' TO APPEAR LIKE A GOOD FELLOW IF I BUY 'EM FROM BRER BEAR WITH TH' SWIPED CHICKEN MONEY!
AWK! WHAT IN TARNATION TH' MONEY'S ALL GONE
POP! I TOLD THEM! AND THEY'RE ALL WAITING!
LI'L WOLF! WHERE'S TH' MONEY THAT WAS IN TH' SUGAR BOWL?
I USED IT, POP, TO BUY THOSE CHICKENS FROM BRER BEAR!
YOU MEAN YOU DIDN'T SWIPE 'EM?
HOW ARE WE GONNA GET MORE CHICKENS? ALL TH' CRITTERS OUT THERE ARE GONNA BE FURIOUS!
I HAPPEN TO KNOW BRER BEAR WANTS SOME POST HOLES DUG! MAYBE... IN EXCHANGE FOR SOME CHICKENS...
Y-YOU MEAN... WORK?
LATER...
THEY'RE ALL HAVING A KEEN TIME, POP... AND THEY EVEN SENT A DRUMSTICK OVER TO YOU!
FOR HE'S A JOLLY GOO FELLOW!
BAH!

WALT DISNEY'S
GRANDMA DUCK
WDC 156-09
GUS GOOSE! I THINK IT'S TIME YOU STARTED PLOWING THAT NORTH FIELD!
YES, MUM!
AND YOU'D BETTER GET THE SACK OF SEED FOR PLANTING! IT'S IN THE LOFT!
ALL RIGHT, GRAN'MA!
I FOUND TH' SEED!
FINE! NOW TOSS THE SACK DOWN HERE!
EEK!
CRACK!
THUD!
LAND SAKES, GUS! WHAT HAPPENED?
I FORGOT TO LET GO OF TH' SACK, MUM!
AND JUST LOOK... YOU'VE BROKEN OUR ONE AND ONLY PLOW!
I DID?
SEED
OH, WELL, IT WASN'T MUCH GOOD ANYHOW!... ONLY PLOWED ONE FURROW AT A TIME!

BUT YOU'LL HAVE TO FIX IT, GUS! WE CAN'T AFFORD TO BUY ANOTHER!
WELL...I'LL TRY!
SHORTLY...
GOODNESS! I HAVEN'T SEEN GUS HOOK UP DOBBIN TO THAT PLOW YET!
GRACIOUS SAKES! THE PLOW IS STILL BROKEN!
GLUE
GUS! WHAT ARE YOU DOING?
PLOWIN' AND PLANTIN' BY HAND, MUM! I COULDN'T FIX THAT OLD PLOW!
SEED
HUMPH! YOU'LL NEVER GET DONE AT THIS RATE! YOU MEN FOLKS JUST DON'T USE YOUR HEADS!
BUT...
FIDDLE FADDLE! I'LL SHOW YOU HOW TO PLOW THIS FIELD TWICE AS FAST AS THAT OLD PLOW EVER DID IT!
?
SEE, GUS? NOW I CAN FINISH MY KNITTING AND PLOW TWO FURROWS AT THE SAME TIME!

WALT DISNEY
PLUTO
in
CHIPMUNK MONKEYSHINES
HORACE HORSECOLLAR IS BUILDING HIS OWN CABIN UP AT THE LAKE! MICKEY'S BEEN HELPING AND PLUTO MAY GET HIS CHANCE TOO!
GOLLY, MICKEY... I HATE TO THINK OF SLEEPING OUT ON THE GROUND TONIGHT... BUT YOU KNOW THESE HILLS ARE FULL OF RASCALS WHO MIGHT STEAL MY LUMBER!
SHUCKS! WE'LL LEAVE PLUTO TO GUARD THINGS, HORACE... AND MY CABIN'S CLOSE BY!
W OS 853-03
O!
REMEMBER... WE'RE DEPENDING ON YOU, PLUTO! SCARE OFF ANY PROWLERS! DON'T LET ANYBODY TAKE ANYTHING!
ARF!
YES, SIR! PLUTO WILL SHOW THEM EVERYTHING IS SAFE WITH HIM ON THE JOB! EVEN WITH THE DARK WOODS ALL AROUND HIM... HE'S NOT AFRAID!
GR-R-R!
UCH, THAT IS!
GULP!
O TELLING WHAT MIGHT BE
URKING OUT IN THOSE WOODS!
THAT'S FOR SURE! LOOK! IT'S THOSE LITTLE BUSY-BODIES, CHIP 'N' DALE!
COME ON, DALE! OVER HERE! LOTS OF THINGS TO CRACK THIS WHOPPER NUT ON!
YEH, YEH! WE PRETTY SMART!
ALL WE NEED IS A GOOD HARD BRICK OR SOMETHING AND THEN WE CAN... WHAM!
PROWLERS... THINKS PLUTO!
UT
E'S
EADY
FOR
HEM!
GR-R-R-R!
LOOK OUT, CHIP... A MONSTER!
!

YEOW!
WHOA, DALE... STOP! WE LEFT OUR YUMMY NUT BACK THERE
WHO CARES!? LET THE MONSTER HAVE IT!
MONSTER PHOOEY! HE JUST A DOG, AND NO DUMBBELL POOCH GONNA KEEP THE BIGGEST NUT WE EVER HAD!
SHHH... NOW WHEN I GET HIS ATTENTION... YOU GRAB OUR NUT... AND RUN!
(GULP!) I WISH I COULD DO THE RUNNING PART RIGHT NOW!
SNIFF!
CHEE! CHEE! ZUT! ZUT!
ARF!?
I'VE GOT IT, CHIP! I'VE GOT IT!
GASP!
THAT'S ALL PLUTO NEEDS TO HEAR! HE DOESN'T KNOW WHAT THEY GOT... BUT THOSE LITTLE RASCALS AREN'T GOING TO GET AWAY WITH IT WHILE HE'S ON THE JOB!
ARF! ARF! ARF!
AND AFTER A LONG HARD CHASE... NOBODY IS MORE SURPRISED THAN PLUTO WHEN...HE ACTUALLY GETS THE THE CULPRITS CORNERED!
OH, NO! DON'T BITE US, BIG FELLA!
WE JUST HAD TO GET BACK OUR PEACHY NUT!
!

JUST A NUT! AND PLUTO FEELS LIKE TWO CENTS!
BIG BULLY! CHASING US POOR LI'L CHIPMUNKS ABOUT OUR VERY OWN NUT!
AW, DON'T BE TOO HARD ON HIM, DALE!
THAT'S THE WAY IT IS WITH WATCHDOGGIES! THEY JUST GUARDS EVERYTHING AROUND THEIR PLACE!
OH! NO BRAIN-WORK, EH?
SPEAKING OF GUARDING... LOOK!
GASP!
HOHO! WE'VE GOT THE BEST STUFF! NOW GET GOING BEFORE THAT DOG COMES BACK!
OH, NO! ALL THIS THIEVERY GOING ON WHILE PLUTO'S OUT CHASING A SILLY NUT!
ARF! ARF! ARF!
YOU'RE TOO LATE, MUTT! HAW, HAW!
POOR PLUTO! AND TO THINK MICKEY AND HORACE TRUSTED HIM TO GUARD THINGS!
OO-OO-OOW..!
GUESS HE JUST A FIZZLER WHEN IT COME TO WATCH-DOGGING!
IT PARTLY OUR FAULT THOUGH!
DALE! DOGGIE! THOSE CROOKS GOTTA DRIVE 'ROUND BY BIG HILL BEND! COME ON! WE CAN BEAT 'EM THERE BY THE SHORT-CUT!
(PUFF, PUFF!) AND WE NOT CHAMPEEN CHEWERS FOR NOTHING!
?
HERE'S A GOOD ROLLER, DALE! START CHEWING THE PROPS OFF!
JUST DO LIKE WE DO, DOGGIE!
CHOMP!
CHOMP!
CHOMP!

THERE SHE GO, POOCHY!
WHEE! JUST IN TIME! HERE COME THE CROOKS...AROUND THE BEND!
KERASH!
YIPPEE! THAT STOPS 'EM FOR YOU, DOGGIE!
EVEN OUT IN THESE PARTS SUCH A RACKET BRINGS FOLKS OUT IN A HURRY!
GR-R-R!
MICKEY! THIS LUMBER IN THEIR TRUCK...IT'S MINE! SEE...HERE ARE THESE RAFTERS WE NOTCHED!
MIGOSH! AT LEAST THEY DIDN'T GET AWAY WITH THEM!
BUT HOW DID THIS LOG GET DOWN HERE? WHEN I CAME BY A FEW MINUTES AGO, THE ROAD WAS CLEAR!
PLUTO! THIS LOG! ...YOU COULDN'T HAVE...YOU DIDN'T ...ER...DID YOU?
ARF! ARF!
AMAZING! HE DID! HE MUST HAVE!
WHAT A...ER ...RESOURCEFUL DOG!
HUMPH! HE THE BIG HERO!
OH, WELL...WE STILL GOT THAT NUT...I HOPE!
BUT PLUTO DOESN'T FORGET WHO WAS REALLY RESPONSIBLE! BRIGHT AND EARLY NEXT DAY...TO SHOW HIS GRATITUDE...
GR-ROOF! M-M-WOOF! URF!
SPEAK UP, DOGGIE! WHAT YOU TRYING TO SAY?
ARF!
OOF! OW! NOW I GET IT!
WHAT HE SAY? WHAT?
NUTS TO US! HEH... MORE, THAT IS!
ARF!

Walt Disney
presents
GOOFY AND Ellsworth
A.K.A. Cormorant Number Twelve
LOOK, ELLSWORTH! I HAD A LI'L EXTRA MONEY, SO I BOUGHT US SOME *SEA BASS* FER DINNER! YUM-*MEEE!*
YOU REALLY LIKE FISH *THAT* MUCH, GOOFY?
J- 517

'COURSE I DO! THEY'RE RICH IN *PHOSPHOROUS,* YUH KNOW!
NOT TO MENTION *SCALES!*

WE TALKING MYNAH BIRDS AREN'T FISH FANATICS! TOO MUCH TROUBLE TO PICK THE BONES OUT!

'COURSE, CATCHING FISH IS WONDERFUL SPORT! LISTEN HERE, GOOF– "CORMORANT FISHING CONTEST TODAY!"
WHUT KINDA FISHIN'?
CORMORANT FISHING! THEY'RE BIG, DOPEY BIRDS THAT DIVE TO CATCH FISH! AND YOU CAN TRAIN THEM TO CATCH 'EM FOR YOU!
HI, GOOFY! HOWDY, ELLSWORTH! HOME-COOKING, EH?
WHERE YUH HEADED, HORACE?
HEY, A CORMORANT! ENTERING THE CONTEST, PAL?
GOOD GUESS! AND MY VICTORY'S A FAIT ACCOMPLI!
I WOULDN'T BE SURPRISED! LOOKS LIKE HE'S GOT A KEEN EYE!
YEP! JUST LIKE ME, HE'S A FISHING CHAMP!
AND HAVE WE WON PRIZES? HAW! BY THE BOATLOAD! HE TIED FOR FIRST IN THE DUSTY LAKE FINALS! THEN WE WENT ON TO THE REGIONALS AT THUNDER BAY, AND AFTER THAT BLAH-BLAH YAKKETY-SHMACKETY...

TOO BAD *YOU* DON'T HAVE A CORMORANT TO WIN *SECOND* PLACE, GOOF!
THET'S OKAY! GOOD LUCK, HORACE!
AND GOOD *FISHING*—
AWK! THAT JAW-GRINDING GLUTTONBIRD GOT A *HEAD START!*
I'LL GO TEACH THAT BUZZARD SOME MANNERS!
LET IT GO, ELLSWORTH! YUH'D JUST MAKE HORACE MAD!
⋟SIGH!⋞ I WAS LOOKIN' FORWARD TO THET DINNER...AN' NOW I'M OUTTA MONEY!
⋟HMM!⋞ THERE'S A BRAINY SOLUTION TO EVERY CRISIS!
I'VE *GOT* IT, GOOFY! WE *WILL* ENTER THAT CORMORANT FISHING CONTEST!
BUT *HOW?*

WE AIN'T GOT A CORMORANT!
WE DO NOW! YOURS TRULY, WITH A DAB OF MAKEUP...
...AND THE REQUIRED RING AROUND THE NECK ‹HACK, CHOKE!› TO KEEP ME FROM SWALLOWING FISH WHOLE–THOUGH JUST THE IDEA MAKES ME QUEASY!
YUH REALLY THINK YUH'LL PASS FER A CORMORANT?
SURE, SILLY! JUST TELL 'EM...‹PSST! PSST!›
HOWDY, STRANGER! SIGNIN' IN, PLEASE, WITH MUH CORMORANT FROM HADACRASHCAR!
‹AHEM!› RRRRIGHT! LOOKS LIKE NO BREED I'VE EVER SEEN!
SIGN HERE AND GO STRAIGHT TO THE CONTEST SITE! IT STARTS IN HALF AN HOUR!
OKEE-DOKE!
WE'RE IN, ELLSWORTH!
YOU REALLY SHOULD HAVE SAID MADAGASCAR, BUT HE BOUGHT IT ANYWAY!

I'LL TAKE CARE OF OUR GEAR, GOOFY! YOU JUST KEEP THE *PEDAL* TO THE METAL!
GOTCHA!
MOUSETON, THE CORMORANT HAS LANDED!
CORMORANT FISHING CONTEST
LOOKIT ALL THUH CONTESTANTS! AN' LOOKIT THUH *POLICE* BOATS OUT THERE, WATCHIN' OVER THINGS!
6
7
8
NUMBER 12? YOUR ROCK IS OVER THERE, SIR!
SAY! IS THERE *ALWAYS* THIS MUCH *SECURITY* AT CORMORANT FISHIN' CONTESTS?
HEH! THOSE POLICE BOATS AREN'T FOR US! THE COPS THINK THERE'S SOME *JEWEL SMUGGLING* GOING ON AROUND HERE, SO THEY'RE KEEPING A CLOSE WATCH ON THE SHORELINE!

SMUGGLING, EH? HMM...
HEY, THERE'S HORACE!
10
AN' TRUDY VAN TUBB!
11
HUH?!?
IT *IS* THE OL' GIRL, WITH A FISH-MANGLER OF HER OWN!
HMM! THAT'S FUNNY! WHO'D THINK *BLACK PETE'S* SNOOTY *MOLL* WENT IN FOR SPORTS LIKE *CORMORANT* *FI—*
KA-WHAM!
OOPS! YUK! DIDN'T SEE THUH POLE!
THAT'S OKAY, ADDLEHEAD! IT HAD YOUR NUMBER, ANYWAY!
12
HEY, YOU UP THERE! NEED SOME HELP?
NO THANKS! NOTHIN'S BROKEN... *YET!*
12

NOW TO PUT ON MY GEAR REAL QUICK!
I'LL COVER YUH! BUT ARE YUH SURE YUH KNOW HOW TA *ACT* LIKE A CORMORANT?
HEH! HAVEN'T I EVER SHOWN YOU MY *SKINDIVING SCHOOL* DIPLOMA?
College of Underwater Knowledge
Bachelor of Subaquatic Arts
CONTESTANTS! GET SET... *GO!!*
JUDGES
AND *I* KNOW EXACTLY *WHERE* TO GO!
HYUCK! I GOTTA GIVE ELLSWORTH CREDIT! HE'S ONE SMART, SMART COOKIE!

THERE'S HORACE'S GREEDY-GUT CORMORANT NOW! HE'S ALREADY MADE A GOOD CATCH!
GIMME THAT! YOU SWIPE FROM ME, I SWIPE FROM YOU!
WHA'? YOU'RE NOT SUPPOSED TO COME UP EMPTY-BEAKED!
YOU'RE S'POSED TO HAVE THE HORSECOLLAR TOUCH! GET BACK DOWN THERE!
SPLASH
BACK AGAIN, EH? SAME FISH-TIME, SAME FISH-CHANNEL! I HATE TO ADMIT IT...BUT HE'S GOOD!
I'LL TAKE THAT, THANK YOU! FISHING IS SUCH A BOTHER, BUT I'M DOING IT FOR GOOFY!

WAIT! TAKE THIS TRIBUTE TO YOUR HORSE-FACED HEADMAN!
CANNED TUNA WITH ONIONS! ARE YOU PULLING MY LEG?
HURRY UP, STUPID! I NEED JUST ONE MORE!
THIS'LL DO JUST FINE! NOW WE'RE EVEN!
HUH?! YOU KNOW I WEAR A SIZE 13! HAVE YOU FLIPPED YOUR FEATHERS?
I'M FLIPPIN' YOU BACK!
WHAP!

NOT BAD! I'VE PICKED UP THREE FISH FOR GOOFY AND TAUGHT THAT DINNER-SNATCHING GLUTTON A LESSON!
OOPS! ANOTHER CORMORANT! LOW BRIDGE, BUSTER!
HOLD THE PHONE! THAT WAS TRUDY'S BIRD! AND HE DROPPED SOMETHING SHINY!
A DIAMOND THE SIZE OF A LEMON!
HERE YOU GO, GOOFY! WILL THIS DO?
YOU BET, ELLSWORTH!
CONTESTANT NO. 10, HORACE HORSECOLLAR, HAS WITHDRAWN FROM THE CONTEST DUE TO TECHNICAL DIFFICULTIES!
GAWRSH! I'M REAL SORRY!

BUT NOW WE CAN LEAVE, TOO! I DON'T CARE ABOUT THUH PRIZE–I'VE GOT THUH FISH I NEED!
AWRIGHT, GOOF! GIVE ME JUST FIVE MORE MINUTES...
OH, AND A FRESH *OXYGEN* BOTTLE! I CRAVE ONE MORE PEEP IN THE DISMAL DEEP!
SWELL!
NOW *REMEMBER,* GOOFY...IF I GIVE *TWO TUGS* ON THE ROPE, PULL THE LINE IN SLOWLY AND HAUL ME UP! GOT IT?
RIGHTY-O, PAL!
HMM! TRUDY'S CORMORANT WENT FOR ANOTHER DIVE!
SNIFF! THIS ONE'S *EMPTY!* THAT *BIRD-BRAIN!*
HERE'S WHERE I CONFIRM A *MAJOR* SUSPICION!
HE'S HEADED WAY OUT TO SEA! CHECK!

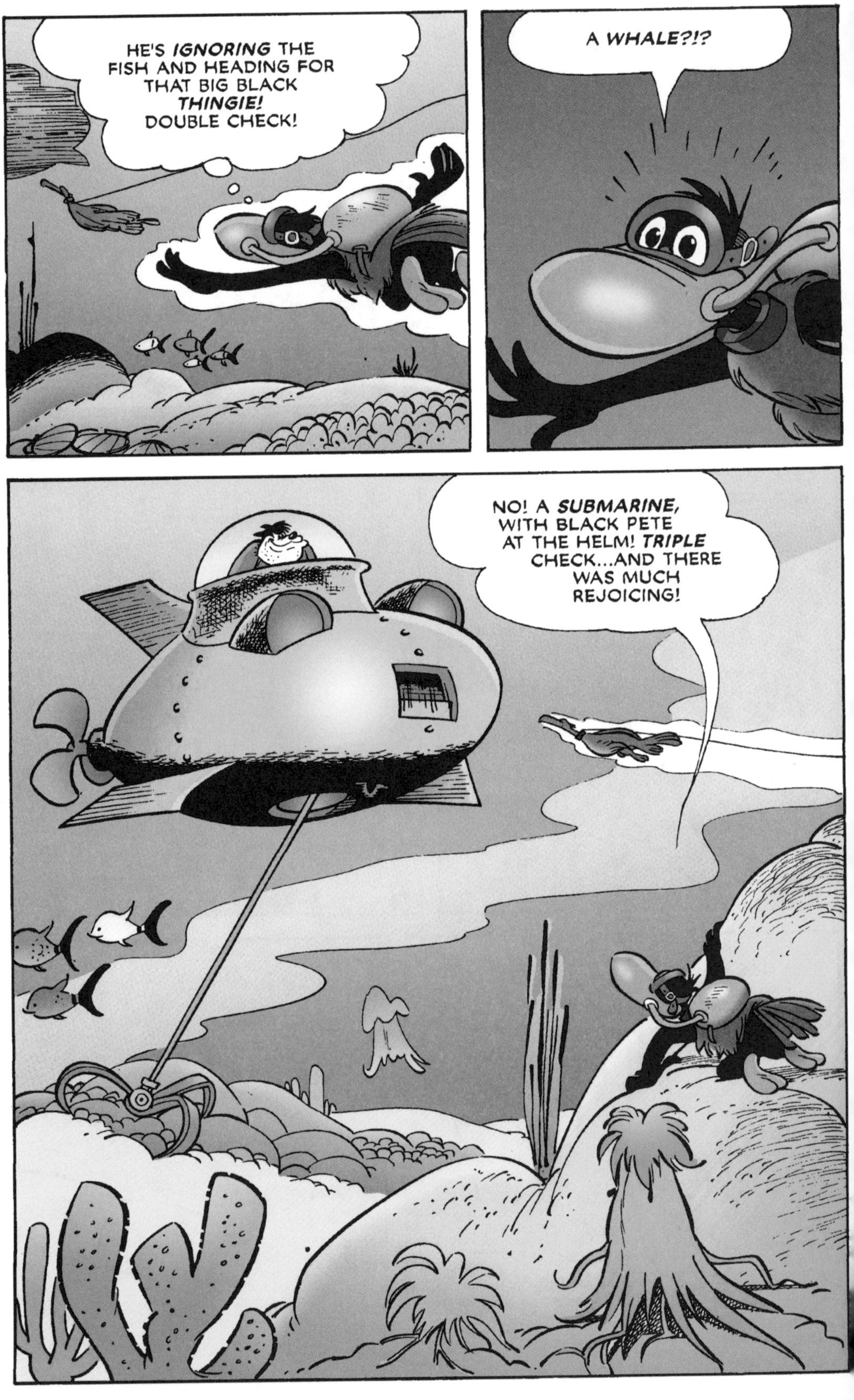
HE'S *IGNORING* THE FISH AND HEADING FOR THAT BIG BLACK *THINGIE!* DOUBLE CHECK!
A *WHALE?!?*
NO! A *SUBMARINE,* WITH BLACK PETE AT THE HELM! *TRIPLE* CHECK...AND THERE WAS MUCH REJOICING!

WHEN I'M RIGHT, I'M RIGHT!
TRUDY'S BIRD IS TRAINED TO GRAB ONLY THE FISH THAT PETE GIVES HIM!
FISH STUFFED WITH DIAMONDS...OOPS! TIME FOR SOME CAMOUFLAGE!
PRETTY SMART PLAN FOR A CLOD LIKE PETE! WITH TRUDY'S HELP, HE'S MOVING THOSE PRICEY BAUBLES RIGHT UNDER THE COPS' BIG NOSES!
JUST LOOK IN THERE...IT'S HALF JEWELRY STORE AND HALF BAIT SHOP!
LAUNCH TUBE

SHALL I *SABOTAGE* THIS CAPER BEFORE THE CORMORANT COMES BACK? WHAT A SILLY QUESTION!
SQRAT
!
THE CABLE CONNECTED TO THIS GRAPPLING HOOK IS BOTH LIGHT *AND* STRONG! THAT GIVES ME AN IDEA!
STEP *A!* JUST WAIT TILL PETE TRIES TO MOVE!
STEP *B!* DEFTLY ATTACH MY *LINE* TO THE HULL...
!
...AND GIVE GOOFY THE *TWO PULLS* WE AGREED ON!
≹AWP!≷ GO PLAY SOMEWHERE ELSE, ESTHER WILLIAMS! I'M KINDA *BUSY* HERE!

TWO PULLS! I'M READIN' YUH LOUD AN' CLEAR, ELLSWORTH! I'LL REEL YUH IN SLOW-LIKE!
ALL I HAVE TO DO NOW IS COME UP BY THE BOATS!
!
I'M BRINGIN' YUH HOME, PAL! SLOW BUT SHURE!
LET'S NOT BRAIN ME WITH THAT LIFE PRESERVER, SHALL WE?
SALUTATIONS, BOYS! I JUST SOLVED YOUR JEWEL SMUGGLING CASE TOOT SWEET!
?
HMPH! THAT YUTZ COULD TANGLE HIS CORMORANT'S LINE UP WITH MINE! I'D BETTER HELP HIM!
OOF! URK! ACK! GAWRSH...

SEE, BUBBY? WITH THIS WOOL-WINDER, YOU CAN REEL IN YOUR LINE REAL EASY!
ACK! OOK! OKAY— URK!
GET IT? NICE AND SIMPLE!
THANKS, MA'AM!
HEY! MUH SUB'S A-MOVIN'! THUH HOOK MUSTA COME LOOSE, AN' THUH CURRENT'S TAKIN' ME TOWARD THUH REEFS!
I'LL TRY THROWIN' 'ER INTO REVERSE—
BLAZES! THUH HOOK WAS CAUGHT IN THE PROPELLER, AN' NOW EVERYTHING'S TORN UP!
I'M DRIFTIN' SHOREWARD! HAS SOME #%$&* GOT IT IN FER ME?

PANT! GASP! GAWRSH, THIS IS HEAVY!
PUFF! WHATCHA ASK YOUR BIRD TO CATCH DOWN THERE, ANYWAY? SHARKS?
I SEE SOMETHING REAL BIG COMING!
I HOPE ELLSWORTH DIDN'T GIT INTO A JAM!
C'MON!
NO, A SEA MONSTER!
NUMBER 12 HAS CAUGHT A GIANT FISH!
LET'S GO LOOK–
TRUDY! YUH GOLDURN OVERSTUFFED NITWIT!
OOH! PETIE! I SO DIDN'T KNOW!
WH- WHUH? WHERE'S ELLSWORTH?

PETE AND VAN TUBB! REACH FOR THE SKY!
YOU'VE SMUGGLED YOUR LAST FISHY DIAMOND!
AND CONGRATULATIONS, MR. GOOF! THAT'S THE BIGGEST CATCH WE'VE EVER SEEN!
OH NO!

AND SO...
HAPPY WITH YOUR FIRST PRIZE MEDAL, GOOFY? NOT EVERYONE WINS A CORMORANT FISHING CONTEST BY LANDING A SUB!
MEBBE NOT, ELLSWORTH! BUT AS FOR MUHSELF, I JUST CAN'T WAIT TO WRAP MUH GUMS AROUND SOME GRILLED SEA BASS!

Walt Disney's
FETHRY DUCK IN
THE RETRIEVER
IF THAT'S COUSIN FETHRY, I WON'T DO IT!
KNOCK! KNOCK!
SOUNDS LIKE A FETHRY KNOCK, AND THAT'S NOT GOOD!
4106
HI, DON! I'M GOIN' DUCK HUNTING!
WAAK!
BUT WHY ME? I'M DOMESTICATED!
NOT YOU! I MEAN REAL DUCKS!
WHAT A SLAP IN THE FACE! WHAT AM I, A FAKE?!
NO— I MEAN MALLARDS, PINTAILS, DUCKS LIKE THAT!
⇒OOH!⇐ I CAN'T BEAR TO LOOK AT HIM!

SO WHAT THE BLAZES ARE YOU DOING HERE?
I JUST WANTED TO ASK YOU...
NO, I ABSOLUTELY WILL NOT GO WITH YOU!
NO, I JUST WANT TO BORROW SOMETHING!
OH, IN THAT CASE, JUST NAME IT— ANYTHING YOU WANT!
ANYTHING TO GET RID OF HIM!
I WANT TO BORROW YOUR RETRIEVER...
WISH HE'D BORROW IT AND LEAVE!
...WHICH IS NONE OTHER THAN TABBY!
REEOWR!
WHAT'S THE MATTER WITH HIM?
HE'S NOT A RETRIEVER— HE'S A CAT!
ACCORDING TO THIS BOOK, "THE CAT IS ONE OF THE GREATEST RETRIEVERS ON THE FACE OF THE EARTH!" BESIDES, YOU SAID I COULD BORROW ANY-THING I ASKED FOR!
ZOO LOGIC
WELL, YOU GOT ME THERE! BUT HOW WILL YOU SELL TABBY ON THE IDEA?
VERY SIMPLE— WATCH THIS! IT SAYS HERE UNDER MALLARDS...

...THAT THEY ARE THE JUICIEST, MOST DELECTABLE OF ALL THE BIRDS!
ZOO LOGIC
BIRDS!?
SEE WHAT I MEAN?
CULINARY PERSUASION! WHO WOULD HAVE THOUGHT?
LET'S GO, BOY! HEEL!
I BETTER ALERT TABBY'S PSYCHIATRIST TO STAND BY!
SO IT'S OFF TO THE HAPPY HUNTING GROUNDS!
I JUST GO FOR THE SPORT! PERSONALLY, I DON'T LIKE DUCK!
H. C. ANDERSEN DUCK LAKE 1 MILE
GLADYS, HERE COMES THAT CRAZY HUNTER AGAIN!

YOU PUT OUT THE DECOYS, I'LL HANDLE THE DISARMAMENT!
THIS CHARACTER NEVER SEEMS TO LEARN!
KEEP YOUR EYES PEELED, RETRIEVER!
THIS IS ONLY HALF THE BATTLE! HE'S STILL GOT TWO LIVE ONES IN THAT RIFLE!
QUIET, TABBY! I HEAR SOMETHING!
DECOYS OUT, GLADYS!
ALL SET! LET'S GO!
QUACK! WAK! HONK!
HONK PFONK! QUACK!
GAME AHOY! BE STILL, MY HEART!

HOW ABOUT THAT! THE PRO-VERBIAL SITTING DUCKS!
BOOM!
OKAY, TABBY! GO GET 'EM!
SO THAT'S WHY I'M HERE!
SWIM IN THAT COLD WATER? HE'S OUT OF HIS FETHRY BRAIN!
OH, NO YOU DON'T! IF YOU THINK YOU JUST CAME FOR THE RIDE, YOU'RE NUTS!
THE BOOK SAYS YOU'RE SUPPOSED TO RETRIEVE! SO RETRIEVE ALREADY!

ONLY TERMITES WOULD LIKE THESE WOODEN-HEADED WADDLERS! THEY'RE COY DECOYS!
AND NOW FOR THE COUP DE GRACE...
A LITTLE VOICE-THROWING! HONK! HAWNK!
THEY'VE GOT YOU SURROUNDED, TABBY! BUT I'LL DEFEND YOU TO THE END!
BLAM!
WHOSE END?! OOH, THAT FETHRY AND HIS FAITH IN BOOKS—
⇒AH!⇐ SAY, FRIEND! HOW'S THE HUNTING?
FABULOUS! I GOT THE LIMIT IN TWO SHOTS!
NO HUNTING!
LATER!
...AND YOU SAY HE SALTED SIX DECOYS AND BARELY MISSED MY CAT? WHAT'S THE BAIL?
NO BAIL! BUT PLEASE, I IMPLORE YOU... PLEASE COME AND GET HIM!
I THINK I'LL TRY AN AFRICAN SAFARI NEXT TIME!

Walt Disney
SUPER GOOF
THE BRAIN FROM N.E.P.H.E.W.
TA-DAH-H! SUPER GOOF TO THUH RESCUE... TA-DAH-H! Z Z Z Z Z Z
UNCLE GOOFY!
W SG 7-03
YOU'VE GOT TO STOP SUPER GOOFING IN YOUR SLEEP WHILE YOU'RE JUST PLAIN GOOFY!
TA...
THUD!
I THINK YOU'VE BEEN WORKING TOO HARD!
I THINK I'VE BEEN SLEEPIN' TOO HARD!
I KNOW... A EUROPEAN TOUR WILL BE JUST THE THING FOR YOU!
ON $1.69 ?
TUT-TUT, DEAR UNCLE... I SHALL BE DELIGHTED TO PAY YOUR WAY OUT OF MY QUIZ SHOW WINNINGS!
HOT DIGGETY... YOU'RE ALL HEART AND BRAINS, GILBERT!

So...
BON VOYAGE, UNCLE GOOFY! RELAX AND HAVE FUN!
BON BYE-BYE TUH YOU, TOO, GENEROUS NEPHEW!
ISN'T IT THRILLING... IN FIVE DAYS WE'LL BE IN ITALY!
FIVE DAYS? THAT'S ALMOST A WEEK!
HOW CAN A FELLER RELAX KNOWIN' HE'S WASTIN' HIS NEPHEW'S MONEY JUST SETTIN' ON A BOAT WASTIN' TIME?
LUCKILY I PACKED SOME GOOBERS...
POING!
TA-DAH-H!
EEK! I FEEL LIKE I'M ON A SPEEDING JET!
SIR... INEXPLICABLE BUT TRUE... WE'RE TRAVELING AT 500 KNOTS!
WE'LL BE IN SUNNY ITALY BEFORE YUH CAN SAY RAVIOLI!
AND SHORTLY...
YUH CAN THANK SUPER GOOF FOR THUH SWIFT VOYAGE! YUK!
LANK!
BOO! THE VOYAGE IS HALF THE FUN!
IT IS?
FUN SQUELCHER!
OUCH!
ZOK!

GUIDED TOUR ... FOLLOW ME!
SAY, I'M IN ON THAT, TOO!
GET OUT YOUR LIGHT METERS...
HUH? WAIT... DON'T TAKE ANY PHOTOS YET!
FLIP!
SUPER GOOF TO THUH RESCUE AGAIN! TA-DAH, AND UPSY-DAISY!
HE STRAIGHTENED THE LEANING TOWER!
BOO!
N SPAIN GOOFY GOOFS AGAIN...
AWRK! THIS IS JUST AWFULLY TURRIBLE!
GLURGH!
SAVED YUH FROM THUH NASTY MAN!
BOO!
FUN FOILER!
FOOEY TO YOUIE!
PUT HEEM DOWN, SEÑOR... OR I WEEL DIE OF DISGRACE!

BAH! C'MON, FOLKS... NEXT STOP, *PARIS, FRANCE!*
AND SO...
THE EIFFEL TOWER!
UH-OH! DOUBLE TROUBLE!
TA-DAH-H...I DON'T WANT TUH GET BLAMED FOR STRAIGHTENING *THIS* TOWER, TOO... SO *THERE!*
CREAK!
AND THEN HALF A MILLION FRENCHMEN DO THE IMPOSSIBLE...
THEY THREW *SUPER GOOF* OUT OF EUROPE!
UNCLE!! BACK SO SOON?!
AND HOW! IT WAS A HORRIBLE HOLIDAY, GILBERT!
BUT WHAT IF YOU DREAM YOU'RE SUPER GOOF AND SLEEP-WALK AGAIN?
I COULD GET SOME NASTY BUMPS DOIN' THAT! HMM...
WHY, THAT'S SUPER SIMPLE, GILBERT! I'M SURPRISED A SMARTY LIKE YOU NEVER THOUGHT OF IT!
I'LL JUST HAVE A SNACK OF GOOBERS AT BEDTIME—BECOME SUPER-TOUGH SUPER GOOF—AND THEN IF I SLEEP-WALK I WON'T HURT MYSELF!

Donald Duck
"SAUCE FOR THE DUCK"
LOOK, KIDS... THE PEWTER POT! THAT RESTAURANT HAS A THREE-STAR RATING IN EATER'S DIGEST!
Pewter Pot
THERE ARE MANY POSH RESTAURANTS IN DUCKBURG, AND DONALD KNOWS THEM ALL—!
H 8011
THERE'S THE COPPER KETTLE! IT WON FOUR STARS FOR CHEF FISHMUCK'S BRINY BOUILLABAISSE!
SIGH! THERE'S THE SILVER SPOON, WHERE THE ELITE EAT UNTIL THEY'RE REPLETE! FIVE STARS!
AND THERE'S THE GOLDEN GOURD! SEVEN STARS FOR ITS EXCLUSIVE ARRAY OF PATÉ GATÉ'! A DIFFERENT GOOSE PASTE FOR EACH DAY OF THE WEEK! SHEER CULINARY BLISS!
BUT THE PLATINUM PAN TOPS THEM ALL! THAT PLACE IS THE NEWEST AND SNOOTIEST IN TOWN! RUMOR HAS IT THEY MAKE A WORLD-CLASS SAUCE!
MAYBE ONE OF THESE DAYS I'LL BE CALLED TO THAT KITCHEN! DONALD DUCK, PURVEYOR OF PRINCELY PROVENDER AND ARTIST IN ANTIPASTO!
MAYBE! RIGHT NOW YOU'RE NEEDED HERE!
HOT DOGS! GETCHER RED HOTS HERE! MUSTARD, ONIONS AND SAU-ER-KRAUT!
EVERY BITE A CULINARY DEEEE-LITE!!
1

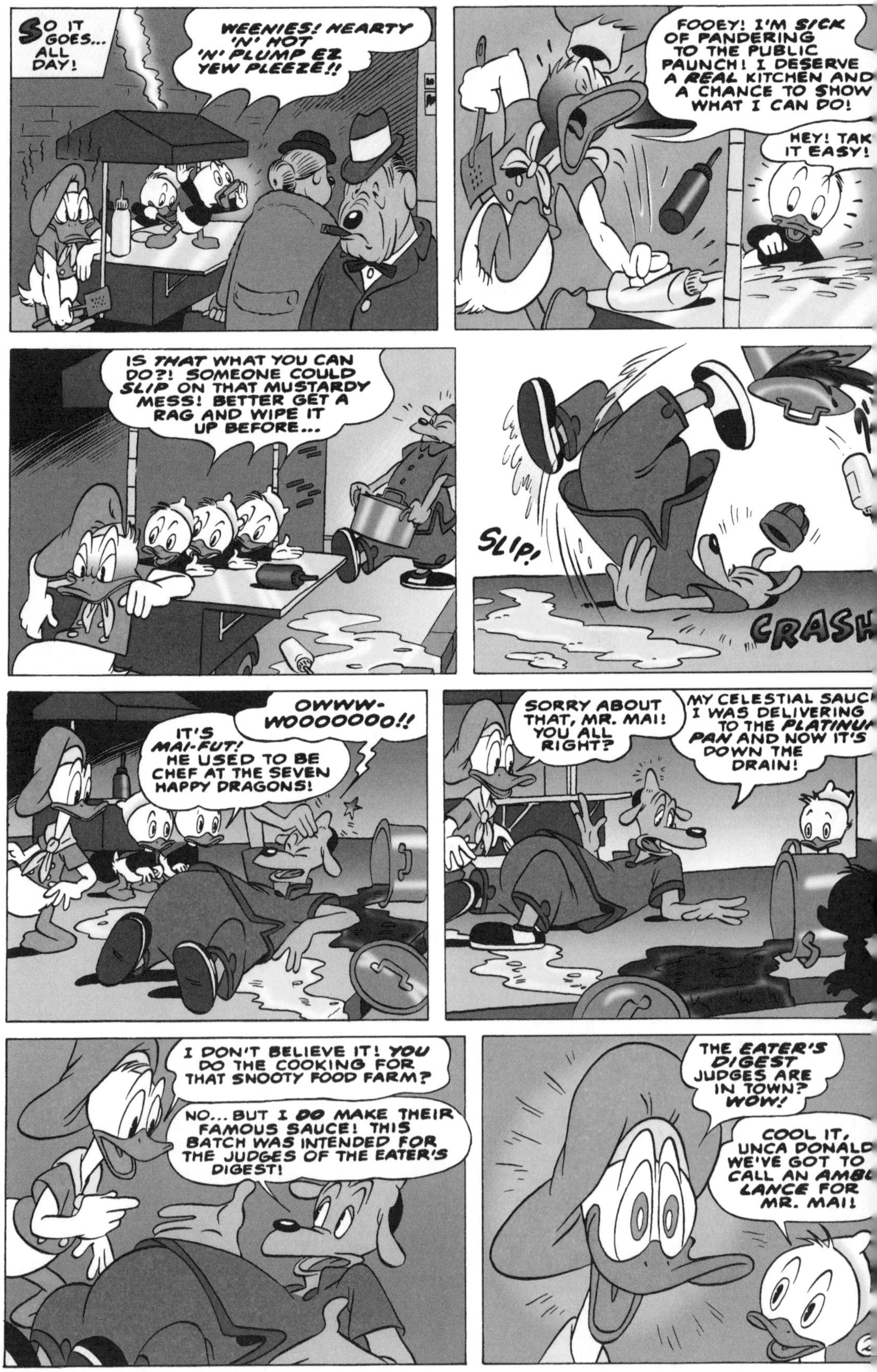
SO IT GOES... ALL DAY!
WEENIES! HEARTY 'N' HOT 'N' PLUMP EZ YEW PLEEZE!!
FOOEY! I'M SICK OF PANDERING TO THE PUBLIC PAUNCH! I DESERVE A REAL KITCHEN AND A CHANCE TO SHOW WHAT I CAN DO!
HEY! TAK IT EASY!
IS THAT WHAT YOU CAN DO?! SOMEONE COULD SLIP ON THAT MUSTARDY MESS! BETTER GET A RAG AND WIPE IT UP BEFORE...
SLIP!
CRASH
OWWW-WOOOOOOO!!
IT'S MAI-FUT! HE USED TO BE CHEF AT THE SEVEN HAPPY DRAGONS!
SORRY ABOUT THAT, MR. MAI! YOU ALL RIGHT?
MY CELESTIAL SAUC I WAS DELIVERING TO THE PLATINU PAN AND NOW IT'S DOWN THE DRAIN!
I DON'T BELIEVE IT! YOU DO THE COOKING FOR THAT SNOOTY FOOD FARM?
NO... BUT I DO MAKE THEIR FAMOUS SAUCE! THIS BATCH WAS INTENDED FOR THE JUDGES OF THE EATER'S DIGEST!
THE EATER'S DIGEST JUDGES ARE IN TOWN? WOW!
COOL IT, UNCA DONALD WE'VE GOT TO CALL AN AMBU LANCE FOR MR. MAI!

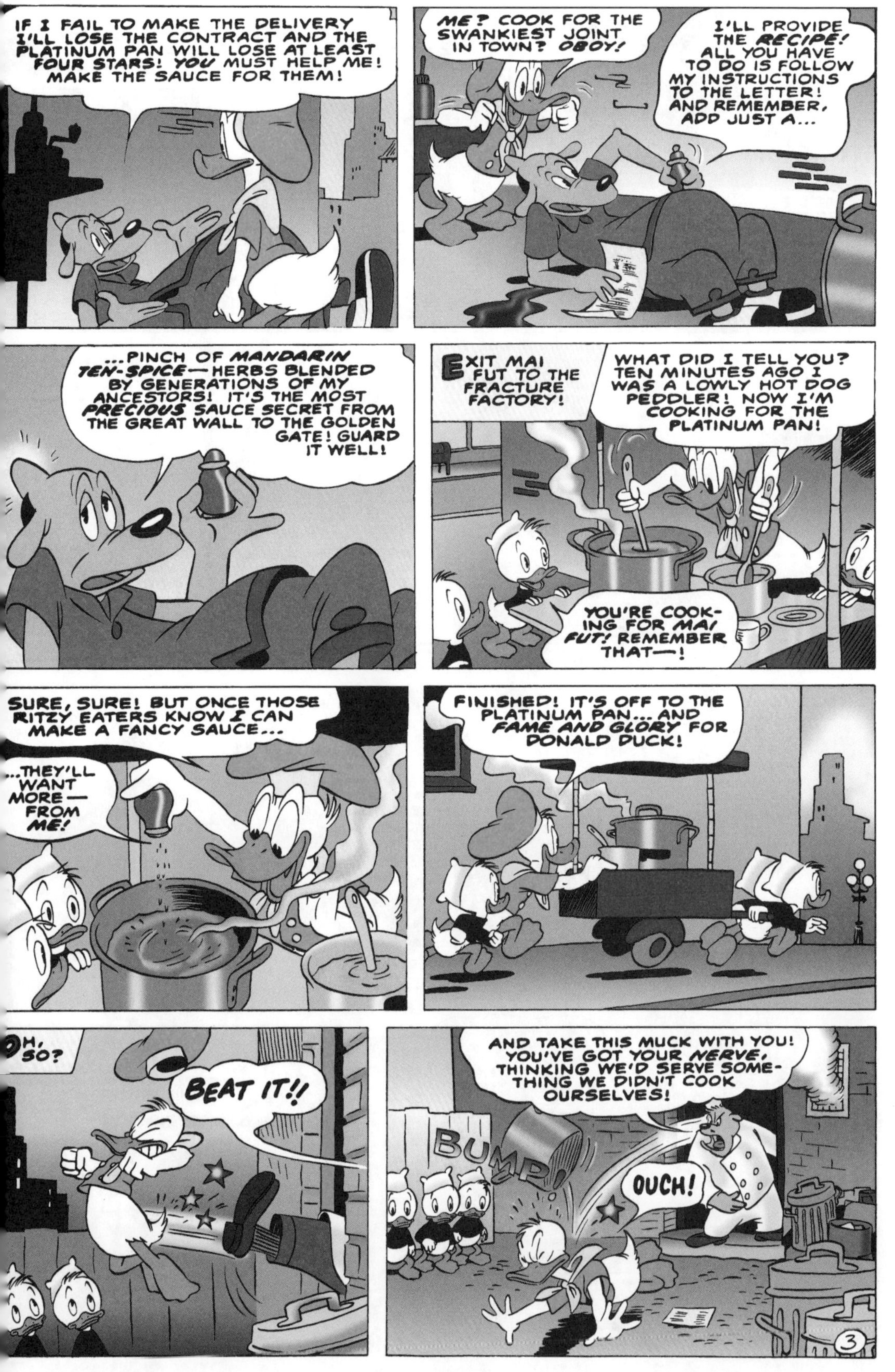
IF I FAIL TO MAKE THE DELIVERY I'LL LOSE THE CONTRACT AND THE PLATINUM PAN WILL LOSE AT LEAST FOUR STARS! YOU MUST HELP ME! MAKE THE SAUCE FOR THEM!
ME? COOK FOR THE SWANKIEST JOINT IN TOWN? OBOY!
I'LL PROVIDE THE RECIPE! ALL YOU HAVE TO DO IS FOLLOW MY INSTRUCTIONS TO THE LETTER! AND REMEMBER, ADD JUST A...
...PINCH OF MANDARIN TEN-SPICE—HERBS BLENDED BY GENERATIONS OF MY ANCESTORS! IT'S THE MOST PRECIOUS SAUCE SECRET FROM THE GREAT WALL TO THE GOLDEN GATE! GUARD IT WELL!
EXIT MAI FUT TO THE FRACTURE FACTORY!
WHAT DID I TELL YOU? TEN MINUTES AGO I WAS A LOWLY HOT DOG PEDDLER! NOW I'M COOKING FOR THE PLATINUM PAN!
YOU'RE COOKING FOR MAI FUT! REMEMBER THAT—!
SURE, SURE! BUT ONCE THOSE RITZY EATERS KNOW I CAN MAKE A FANCY SAUCE...
...THEY'LL WANT MORE—FROM ME!
FINISHED! IT'S OFF TO THE PLATINUM PAN... AND FAME AND GLORY FOR DONALD DUCK!
OH, SO?
BEAT IT!!
AND TAKE THIS MUCK WITH YOU! YOU'VE GOT YOUR NERVE, THINKING WE'D SERVE SOMETHING WE DIDN'T COOK OURSELVES!
BUMP
OUCH!
3

BUT THIS IS THE GENUINE CELESTIAL SAUCE!
SCRAM! GO BACK TO YOUR HOT DOGS!
GARBAGE RATING: 8 STARS
THAT FIGURES! THE CHEF MUST HAVE SEEN OUR CART IN THE STREET—OR TASTED ONE OF OUR PTOMAINE SPECIALS!
HE'LL NEVER BELIEVE WE'RE COLLABORATING WITH MAI FUT ON A GOURMET SAUCE!
MAYBE IF UNCA DONALD LEARNED CHINESE REAL QUICK...
WHAT'LL YOU DO NOW, UNCA DONALD?
WHAT ANY GOOD COOK WOULD DO! I'LL MAKE THEM EAT THEIR WORDS!
SOON, OUTSIDE THE GREASY GRIDDLE...
LEMME GET THIS STRAIGHT...YOU'RE GIVING ME THAT SAUCE? WHAT'S THE CATCH?
Help Your-Self!
NO CATCH! JUST THOUGHT YOU'D LIKE TO ADD SOME VARIETY TO YOUR MENU!
HMM...FOLKS HAVE BEEN COMPLAINING ABOUT THE GRUB LATELY! IT COULDN'T HURT TO TRY SOME-THING NEW! YOU'RE ON, DUCK!
HEE-HEE! WAIT TILL THE PLATINUM PAN LEARNS THAT THE SAUCE THEY COCKED THEIR SNIFFY NOSES AT IS MAKING THE GREASY GRIDDLE A SUCCESS!
THAT'LL GIVE 'EM FOOD FOR THOUGHT!
AN HOUR LATER!
...THE GREASY GRIDDLE! MUST WE STOP HERE? I DISTINCTLY RE-CALL A MAMMOTH CASE OF HEART-BURN!
CAN'T BE HELPED! LAST YEAR'S PANEL GAVE THE PLACE A STAR FOR QUAINT-NESS, AND IT'S OUR DUTY TO REVIEW THAT RATING! GIRD YOUR STOMACHS, GENTLEMEN!
Eater's DIGEST
BUT IT'S SPLENDID! A SAUCE FIT FOR THE GODS!
NO DOUBT THEY HAVE A NEW CHEF! I PROPOSE WE GIVE THIS JEWEL OF AN EATERY FOUR STARS! ALL IN FAVOR—?
AYE! AYE

AND SO...
MR. DUCK! MASTER DUCK! YOU'RE A TRUE CHEF, AND YOUR SAUCE WAS A HOWLING SUCCESS!!
EATER'S DIGEST HAS QUADRUPLED MY RATING! COME WORK IN MY FOUR-STAR PALACE! TOGETHER WE'LL MAKE A FORTUNE... A REAL AFTER-DINNER MINT!
NO THANKS! I'VE SET MY SIGHTS ON HIGHER STARS!
WORD OF DONALD'S SUCCESS SPREADS LIKE SYRUP ON A TABLE-CLOTH...
DID YOU HEAR? THE GRIDDLE SNAGGED FOUR STARS THANKS TO SOME GUY CALLED DUCK!
The Watched POT
YOU DON'T SAY! I KNOW A HOT DOG VENDOR NAMED DONALD DUCK...
BY MORN-ING!
COME WORK FOR THE COPPER KETTLE! WE'LL REMODEL OUR KITCHEN FOR YOU!
THE PEWTER POT WILL DO BETTER THAN THAT! WE'LL PAY YOU!
BUT THE SILVER SPOON SEEKS YOUR SUCCULENT SAUCE!
ONE SIDE, PEASANTS! I, CHEF AURIC OF THE GOLDEN GOURD, OFFER THIS DUCK MY PATRONAGE—AND THE MYRIAD SECRETS OF MY PATE' BUFFET!
GENTLEMEN, PLEASE! YOU CAN ALL HAVE A TUB OF MY SAUCE... GRATIS!
THE GOLDEN GOURD! WHEN THAT SEVEN-STAR CHEF COMES BEGGING, YOU KNOW YOU'VE ARRIVED!
MAYBE! BUT WE'RE HOLDING OUT FOR FIRST PLACE... WITH THE ONE RESTAURANT THAT REALLY COUNTS!
IN THE FRAGRANT KITCHEN OF THE PLATINUM PAN...
WORD HAS REACHED MY EAR THAT SOME UPSTART NAMED DUCK IS DISTRIBUTING SAUCE ALL OVER TOWN... OUR CELESTIAL SAUCE! I DON'T SUPPOSE HE CAME HERE YESTERDAY—??
=GULP!= HE DID, YOUR LORD-SHIP!
5

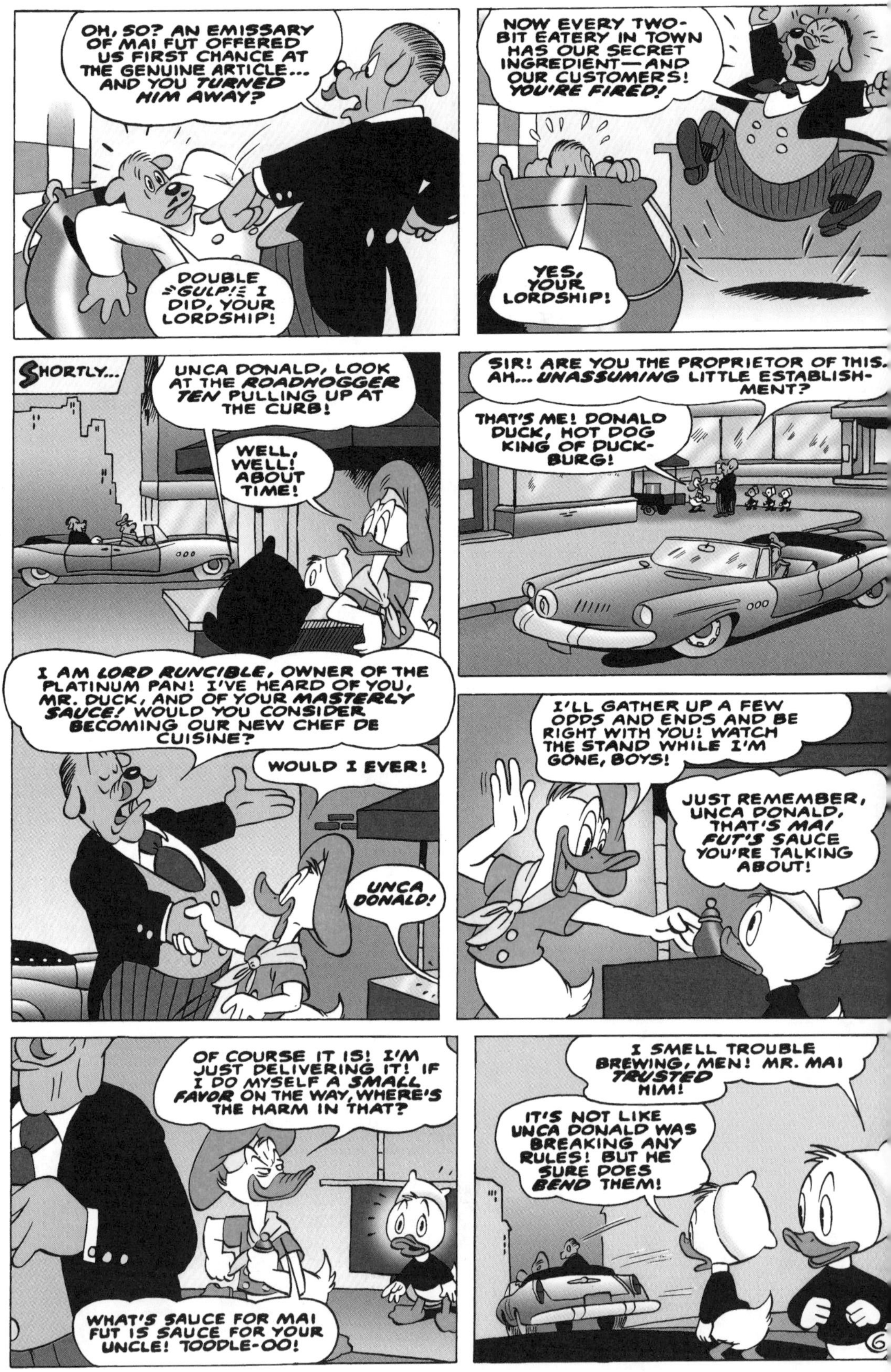
OH, SO? AN EMISSARY OF MAI FUT OFFERED US FIRST CHANCE AT THE GENUINE ARTICLE... AND YOU TURNED HIM AWAY?
DOUBLE GULP! I DID, YOUR LORDSHIP!
NOW EVERY TWO-BIT EATERY IN TOWN HAS OUR SECRET INGREDIENT—AND OUR CUSTOMERS! YOU'RE FIRED!
YES, YOUR LORDSHIP!
SHORTLY...
UNCA DONALD, LOOK AT THE ROADHOGGER TEN PULLING UP AT THE CURB!
WELL, WELL! ABOUT TIME!
SIR! ARE YOU THE PROPRIETOR OF THIS... AH... UNASSUMING LITTLE ESTABLISHMENT?
THAT'S ME! DONALD DUCK, HOT DOG KING OF DUCKBURG!
I AM LORD RUNCIBLE, OWNER OF THE PLATINUM PAN! I'VE HEARD OF YOU, MR. DUCK, AND OF YOUR MASTERLY SAUCE! WOULD YOU CONSIDER BECOMING OUR NEW CHEF DE CUISINE?
WOULD I EVER!
UNCA DONALD!
I'LL GATHER UP A FEW ODDS AND ENDS AND BE RIGHT WITH YOU! WATCH THE STAND WHILE I'M GONE, BOYS!
JUST REMEMBER, UNCA DONALD, THAT'S MAI FUT'S SAUCE YOU'RE TALKING ABOUT!
OF COURSE IT IS! I'M JUST DELIVERING IT! IF I DO MYSELF A SMALL FAVOR ON THE WAY, WHERE'S THE HARM IN THAT?
WHAT'S SAUCE FOR MAI FUT IS SAUCE FOR YOUR UNCLE! TOODLE-OO!
I SMELL TROUBLE BREWING, MEN! MR. MAI TRUSTED HIM!
IT'S NOT LIKE UNCA DONALD WAS BREAKING ANY RULES! BUT HE SURE DOES BEND THEM!
6

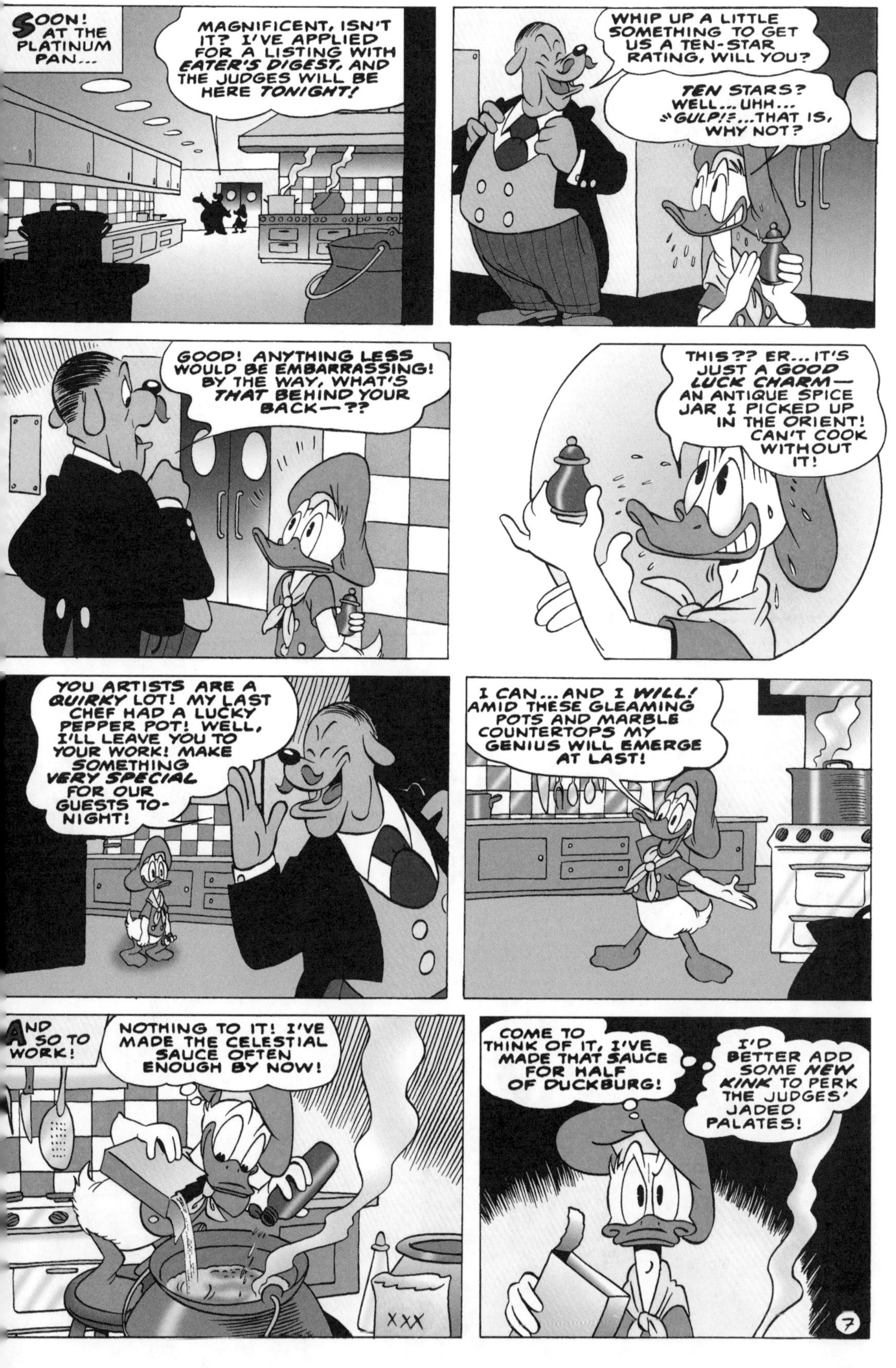
SOON! AT THE PLATINUM PAN...
MAGNIFICENT, ISN'T IT? I'VE APPLIED FOR A LISTING WITH EATER'S DIGEST, AND THE JUDGES WILL BE HERE TONIGHT!
WHIP UP A LITTLE SOMETHING TO GET US A TEN-STAR RATING, WILL YOU?
TEN STARS? WELL... UHH... *GULP!*...THAT IS, WHY NOT?
GOOD! ANYTHING LESS WOULD BE EMBARRASSING! BY THE WAY, WHAT'S THAT BEHIND YOUR BACK—??
THIS?? ER... IT'S JUST A GOOD LUCK CHARM— AN ANTIQUE SPICE JAR I PICKED UP IN THE ORIENT! CAN'T COOK WITHOUT IT!
YOU ARTISTS ARE A QUIRKY LOT! MY LAST CHEF HAD A LUCKY PEPPER POT! WELL, I'LL LEAVE YOU TO YOUR WORK! MAKE SOMETHING VERY SPECIAL FOR OUR GUESTS TO-NIGHT!
I CAN... AND I WILL! AMID THESE GLEAMING POTS AND MARBLE COUNTERTOPS MY GENIUS WILL EMERGE AT LAST!
AND SO TO WORK!
NOTHING TO IT! I'VE MADE THE CELESTIAL SAUCE OFTEN ENOUGH BY NOW!
XXX
COME TO THINK OF IT, I'VE MADE THAT SAUCE FOR HALF OF DUCKBURG!
I'D BETTER ADD SOME NEW KINK TO PERK THE JUDGES' JADED PALATES!
7

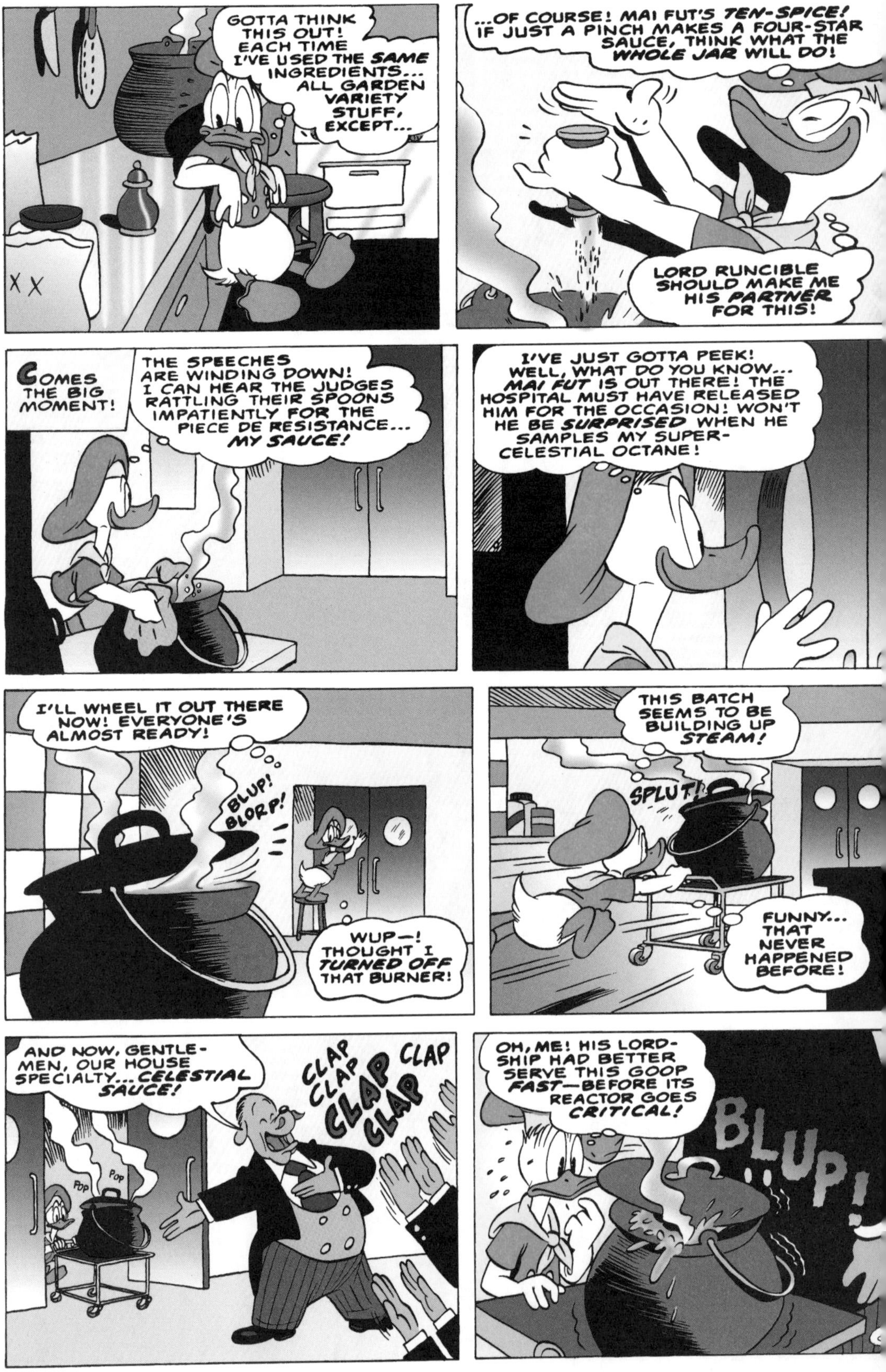
GOTTA THINK THIS OUT! EACH TIME I'VE USED THE SAME INGREDIENTS... ALL GARDEN VARIETY STUFF, EXCEPT...
...OF COURSE! MAI FUT'S TEN-SPICE! IF JUST A PINCH MAKES A FOUR-STAR SAUCE, THINK WHAT THE WHOLE JAR WILL DO!
LORD RUNCIBLE SHOULD MAKE ME HIS PARTNER FOR THIS!
COMES THE BIG MOMENT!
THE SPEECHES ARE WINDING DOWN! I CAN HEAR THE JUDGES RATTLING THEIR SPOONS IMPATIENTLY FOR THE PIECE DE RESISTANCE... MY SAUCE!
I'VE JUST GOTTA PEEK! WELL, WHAT DO YOU KNOW... MAI FUT IS OUT THERE! THE HOSPITAL MUST HAVE RELEASED HIM FOR THE OCCASION! WON'T HE BE SURPRISED WHEN HE SAMPLES MY SUPER-CELESTIAL OCTANE!
I'LL WHEEL IT OUT THERE NOW! EVERYONE'S ALMOST READY!
BLUP! BLORP!
WUP—! THOUGHT I TURNED OFF THAT BURNER!
THIS BATCH SEEMS TO BE BUILDING UP STEAM!
SPLUT!
FUNNY... THAT NEVER HAPPENED BEFORE!
AND NOW, GENTLEMEN, OUR HOUSE SPECIALTY... CELESTIAL SAUCE!
CLAP CLAP CLAP CLAP CLAP
POP POP
OH, ME! HIS LORDSHIP HAD BETTER SERVE THIS GOOP FAST—BEFORE ITS REACTOR GOES CRITICAL!
BLUP!

YOUR PLATE FIRST, SIR NEVILLE... HUH--?!
???
AN HORS D'OEUVRE THAT SERVES ITSELF...?
MOST UN-USUAL!
WATCH OUT!
SPLAT
HORS D'OEUVRES? MORE LIKE CHINESE FIREWORKS!
OR AN ARTILLERY RANGE! TAKE COVER!
POP
PLOP!
MY CELESTIAL SAUCE! WHAT HAVE YOU DONE WITH IT?!
GENTLE-MEN, PLEASE! CALM YOURSELVES!
BAM!
STOP! WAIT! COME BACK!
NOT LIKELY, SIR RUNCIBLE! YOUR SAUCE IS A TRIFLE TOO LIVELY!
POP!
SPLAT!
OUCH! AND HOW!
POP!
FOR TWENTY YEARS I'VE PURSUED EXOTIC FOODS! THIS IS THE FIRST TIME THEY'VE COME CHASING ME!!
BOF!
9

THIS DEBACLE IS AN AFFRONT TO THE ENTIRE GOURMET WORLD! THERE'LL BE NO LISTING FOR THE PLATINUM PAN IN EATER'S DIGEST! WHEN WE'RE FINISHED WITH YOUR LORDSHIP'S REPUTATION, YOU'LL BE LUCKY TO GET A JOB PEDDLING POPSICLES IN THE SAHARA! GOOD DAY, SIR!
HOW CAN THIS BE? WE RUNCIBLES HAVE LED THE CULINARY WORLD SINCE THE TIME OF CHARLEMAGNE!
BOO-HOO! WHAT ABOUT ME? MY ANCESTORS DELIGHTED IMPERIAL TASTE BUDS CENTURIES BEFORE THEN!
I DON'T GET IT! SOMETHING IN THESE HERBS MUST BECOME COMBUSTIBLE WHEN USED IN LARGE QUANTITIES!
SO IT'S YOUR FAULT! YOU EXPLODED MY BANQUET AND MY GOOD NAME! FETCH THE SAUCE KETTLE, MAI FUT! WE'RE GOING TO GIVE THIS VILLAIN A TASTE OF HIS OWN COOKING!
LATER!
I'M DISGRACED! THIS MORNING I WAS TOP CAT ON THE CULINARY SCENE! NOW I LOOK LIKE SOMETHING THE CAT DRAGGED IN!
I'LL CHANGE MY NAME AND MOVE TO TIBET... HEY! WHAT'S THAT CROWD DOING AT MY STAND—?
YOU MISSED A LOT OF EXCITEMENT, UNCA DONALD! OUR HOT DOGS HAVE BEEN SELLING LIKE HOTCAKES! ALL THANKS TO THREE CUSTOMERS...
THREE MESSY-LOOKING GENTS WHO TASTED OUR WARES AND GAVE US TEN GOLD STARS! SAID IT WAS THE FIRST HONEST MEAL THEY'D EATEN ALL WEEK!

WALT DISNEY
JOSÉ CARIOCA in END of the LINE
WAKEY-WAKEY, JOSÉ! IT'S TIME TO CATCH THE FISHES!
B 800011
JOSÉ! IT'S AFTER ELEVEN OF THE CLOCK! WAKE OP!
KNOCK
KNOCK! KNOCK!
HM! NO ANSWERING! IS HE PERHAPS BEING SICK?
HEY, NESTOR! I'M RICH! I'VE FOUND A JOB THAT'S A PIECE OF TORTA!
A JOB? HIM? NOW I KNOW HE IS SICK!
WHAT ABOUT OUR FISHING, JOSÉ?
FORGET FISHING! WITH THE MONEY I AM MAKING, WE'LL BE ABLE TO BUY LOTS OF SARDINHAS IN THE CANS!

WHAT KIND OF WORK COULD BE SO EASY THAT EVEN YOU DO IT?
SEE? I MADE FIFTY SMACKERS IN THREE HOURS! WHAT IS MY WORK, YOU WANT TO KNOW? WELL, I SELL MY PLACE IN LINE!
WHAT LINE?
ANY LINE! THE SHORTAGES IN RIO TODAY MEAN THERE IS A QUEUE FOR EVERYTHING... MOVIES, MEAT, DRIVER'S LICENSES! I JUST GET INTO A LINE— THEN AN HOUR OR TWO LATER, AS I NEAR THE FRONT, I SELL MY PLACE!
THE BUYER GETS TO SKIP TO THE FRONT WITHOUT WAITING! PEOPLE PAY THE GOOD MONEY FOR THAT! COME, I GIVE YOU A GLASS OF WATER AT NO CHARGE!
YOU'RE TOO KIND!
LATER, IN TOWN!
DIDN'T I SAY THERE WAS A LINE FOR EVERYTHING NOW?
HI, JOSÉ!
LOTTERY TICKETS
SEE? THAT FELLOW SELLS THE PLACES IN LINE, TOO! AND, SINCE TODAY IS THE LAST DAY FOR BETTING IN THE LOTTERY, HE HAS MANY CUSTOMERS!
A BUS TICKET LINE! THAT ONE IS FOR ME! I SEE YOU LATER, NESTOR!
BUS STATION
BOARDING

GAROTA DE PANE
SANTA RUMBA
RIO DA SAMBA
BOSSA NOVA
THE LINE OF CUSTOMERS FOR BOSSA NOVA IS THE LONGEST! AND THE PEOPLE ARE LOOKING IN A HURRY!
AN HOUR LATER...
SAY, COULD YOU HOLD MY PLACE? I'LL BE RIGHT BACK!
SURE!
...SO I AM AT THE FRONT OF THE LINE, AND I HEAR TICKETS FOR THE BUS WILL SOON RUN OUT! FOR THIRTY CRUZEIROS I WILL SELL MY PLACE!
DEAL!
MY LEGS ARE NOT YET TIRED! I THINK I WILL FIND ANOTHER LINE!
GOODNESS! JOSÉ IS IN THE LINE FOR BUYING MEAT! DID HE HIT BIG IN THE LOTTERY?
MEAT MARKET
IF HE IS SO WELL OFF, HE CAN AFFORD TO PAY ME THE DINHEIRO HE'S OWED ME FOR A YEAR!
OH, CARLOS, DOESN'T JOSÉ OWE YOU MONEY? HE IS NOW RICH!
RICH?! HE IS OWING ME FIVE SMACKERS!

NOW WE WILL MAKE HIM PAY UP! HE IS IN THE LINE AT THE BUTCHER'S!
HARD TO BELIEVE!
OUGH!
OUGH!
HEY! WHERE'S JOSÉ NOW? HE WAS RIGHT HERE...
MEAT MARKET
BUT HE ISN'T INSIDE!
WOW! ONE HUN-DRED BIG ONES!
CLAUDIAO, HAVE YOU SEEN JOSÉ? HE HAS STRUCK IT RICH!
RICH? NOW HE CAN PAY ME THE FIFTEEN SIMOLEONS HE'S OWED ME FOR AN AGE!
ANOTHER LINE! AND THIS ONE IS LONG! I'LL FINISH THE DAY WITH IT!
SAY, WHAT IS THIS LINE FOR?
IT'S A LINE FOR...
...COLLECTING FROM JOSÉ CARIOCA! HEY! IT'S HIM!
WOW!
CATCH HIM!
AWP! THIS IS THE END OF THE LINE FOR ME!
HE'S RICH!
THE END

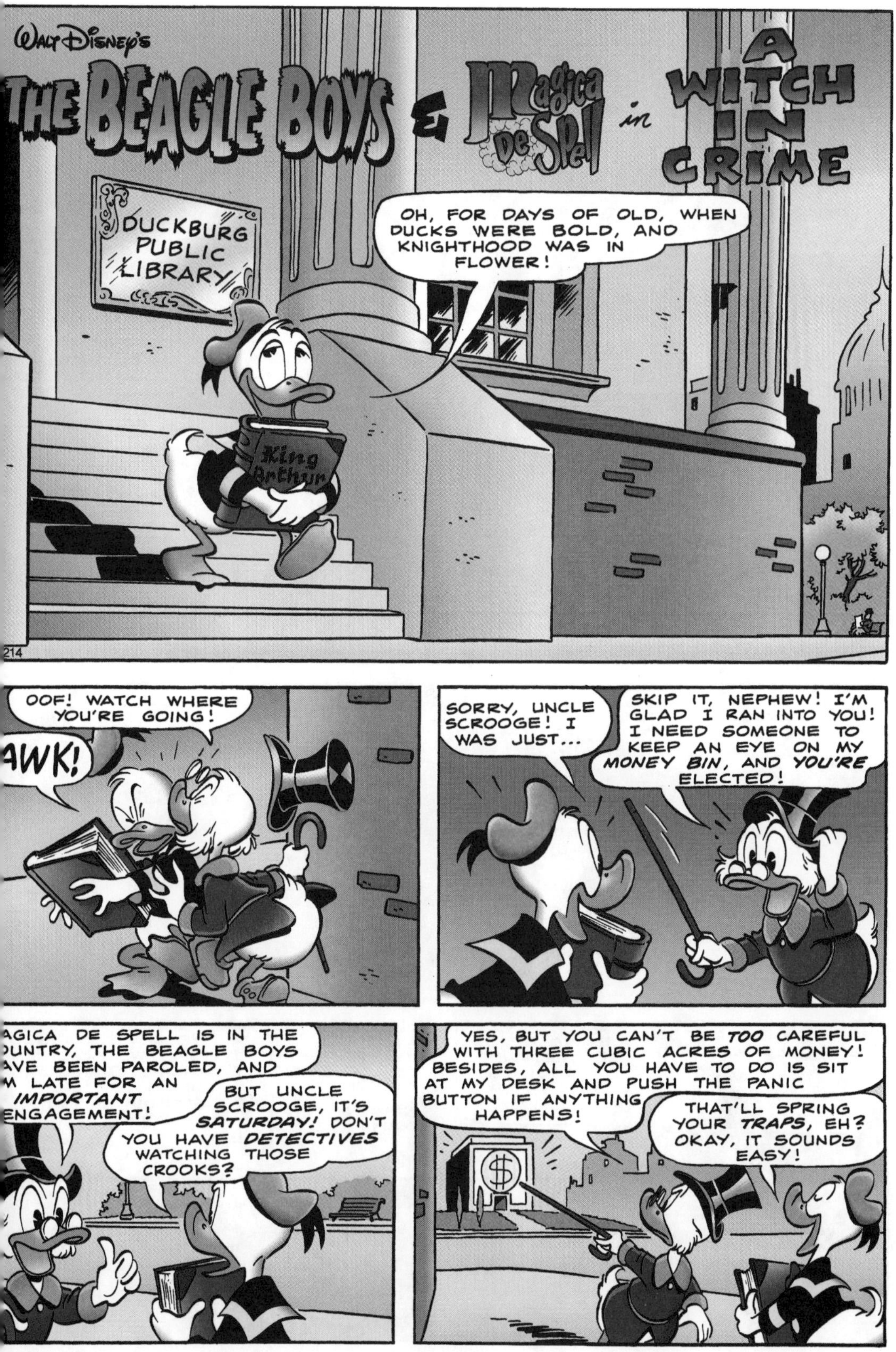

WALT DISNEY'S
THE BEAGLE BOYS & Magica De Spell in A WITCH IN CRIME
DUCKBURG PUBLIC LIBRARY
OH, FOR DAYS OF OLD, WHEN DUCKS WERE BOLD, AND KNIGHTHOOD WAS IN FLOWER!
King Arthur
214
OOF! WATCH WHERE YOU'RE GOING!
AWK!
SORRY, UNCLE SCROOGE! I WAS JUST...
SKIP IT, NEPHEW! I'M GLAD I RAN INTO YOU! I NEED SOMEONE TO KEEP AN EYE ON MY MONEY BIN, AND YOU'RE ELECTED!
AGICA DE SPELL IS IN THE OUNTRY, THE BEAGLE BOYS AVE BEEN PAROLED, AND M LATE FOR AN IMPORTANT ENGAGEMENT!
BUT UNCLE SCROOGE, IT'S SATURDAY! DON'T YOU HAVE DETECTIVES WATCHING THOSE CROOKS?
YES, BUT YOU CAN'T BE TOO CAREFUL WITH THREE CUBIC ACRES OF MONEY! BESIDES, ALL YOU HAVE TO DO IS SIT AT MY DESK AND PUSH THE PANIC BUTTON IF ANYTHING HAPPENS!
THAT'LL SPRING YOUR TRAPS, EH? OKAY, IT SOUNDS EASY!

MEANWHILE, IN A DESERTED MANSION ON THE OUTSKIRTS OF TOWN...
McDUCK'S SNOOPY DETECTIVES THINK THEY'VE GOT ME CORNERED, BUT THANKS TO MY NEW WAND...
...GIVING THEM THE SLIP WILL BE AS EASY AS: "VINES AND TENDRILS, START TO GROW...
"...KEEP THEM HERE WHILE OFF I GO!"
GROAN! WE CAN'T EVEN WARN MR. McDUCK!
THAT'S THE IDEA DEARIES! BUT DON WORRY, I'LL GIVE THE OLD MISER YOUR REGARDS...
...RIGHT AFTER I RELIEVE HIM OF A CERTAIN FIRST DIME! HEE! HEE! HEE!
ON THE OTHER SIDE OF THE TRACKS...
BROTHERS, I SPY A COUPLE OF PRIVATE EYES!
176-671
DO YOU THINK ONE OF US SHOULD WATCH THE BACK OF THEIR SHACK?
NO NEED! THE FRONT DOOR IS THE ONLY WAY OUT OF THAT DUMP!
GUESS IT'S TIME TO USE THE EMERGENCY EXIT!
YEAH! IT'S A GOOD THING WE PRACTICED DIGGING TUNNELS DURING OUR LAST STRETCH IN THE POKEY!
176-671

I'M ALMOST SORRY WE WERE PAROLED BEFORE FINISHING OUR TUNNEL THERE! IT WAS A BEAUT!
HA! ONCE WE SWIPE SCROOGEY'S DOUGH, WE'LL BUY THE JOINT AND MAKE THE WARDEN FINISH IT!
176-671
176-167
THOSE GUMSHOES DON'T EVEN KNOW WE'RE GONE!
THEN LET'S HOP IN THE TRUCK AND GET OUT OF HERE BEFORE THEY WISE UP!
176-167
OVER AT THE ILLIONAIRES' CLUB...
WITH DONALD HOLDING DOWN THE FORT, I CAN RELAX AND ENJOY MY FREE LUNCH!
BUT, BACK AT THE BIN, DONALD'S IN REAMLAND...
BEGONE, EVIL WITCH! I BANISH YOU TO THE BOONIES!
CURSES! MAGIC HAS NO EFFECT ON ONE SO PURE!
AND A REAL SORCERESS HAS ARRIVED...
THIS IS THE LAST TIME I'LL HAVE TO FLY BY BROOM!
FROM NOW ON IT'S LEAR JETS AND HELICOPTERS FOR ME!
McDUCK'S DIME WILL BE MY TICKET TO THE GOOD LIFE! HIGH SOCIETY, HERE I COME!
GASP! THOSE TREES ARE WALKING! IS THERE ANOTHER SORCERESS IN TOWN?

OHO! LEGS! THIS ISN'T SORCERY--IT'S SKULLDUGGERY!
CLOSE ENOUGH, MEN! BREAK OUT THE TOOLS!
HMPH! THOS BUNGLERS HAD BETTER NOT GET IN MY WAY!
176-167
CHECK OUT THIS DIAMOND-TIPPED DRILL! IT'LL BORE THROUGH THE VAULT DOOR IN NOTHING FLAT!
6-671
167
176-761
WAIT! THIS LOOKS LIKE AN ALARM CABLE! I'D BETTER CUT IT FIRST!
76-671
HOW DUMB CAN THEY BE? CUTTING THAT CABLE WILL SET OFF THE ALARM! I'D BETTER DO SOMETHING TO STOP THEM!
BUT FIRST, A QUICK DISGUISE! AH! NOW THEY'LL THINK I'M A MEMBER OF THEIR MORONIC GANG!
POOF!
176-276
HOLD IT, BROTHER! WHY ARE WE DOING THIS THE HARD WAY?
LET'S JUST GO IN THE BACK DOOR! McDUCK WAS TOO CHEAP TO INSTALL AN ALARM THERE!
HE'S RIGHT! THAT WOULD BE MUCH EASIER!
WE SHOULD HAVE THOUGHT OF IT BEFORE!
176-276

HEE HEE HEE! WITH THOSE BOOBS OUT OF THE WAY, I CAN PUT MY OWN PLAN INTO ACTION!
76-276
HEY! WAIT A MINUTE! THE MONEY BIN DOESN'T HAVE A BACK DOOR!
176-671
176-761
176-167
WHICH ONE OF YOU LAMEBRAINS CAME UP WITH THIS DUMB IDEA?
NOT ME!
ME EITHER!
176-761
176-167
HMM! IT WASN'T ME, AND ALL THREE OF US ARE HERE!
COME TO THINK OF IT, ONE OF US STAYED BEHIND AT THE BIN'S ENTRANCE!
176-671
ALL RIGHT, BUDDY! WHO ARE YOU?
WHY...ER...I'M YOUR COUSIN FROM THE GOOSETOWN BRANCH! I CAME TO HELP YOU OUT ON THIS JOB!
6-276
NO WAY! BEAGLE BOYS BY-LAWS CLEARLY STATE THE BIN IS OURS! GO FIND YOUR OWN PIGEON!
OH, PIFFLE! ENOUGH OF THIS NONSENSE!
6-167
176-671
-761
276
AND ENOUGH OF THIS STUPID DISGUISE!
POOF!
GULP! MAGICA DE SPELL!
THAT'S RIGHT! AND YOU BEAGLES ARE INTERFERRING WITH MY PLANS TO PLUCK McDUCK! SO SCRAM!

NO WAY, SISTER! WE WERE HERE FIRST! YOU GO!
176-167
176-671
176-761
SCREECH! YOU DARE TO ORDER ME AROUND?
I'LL SHOW YOU THAT BEAGLE BRAWN IS NO MATCH FOR THE SPELLS OF CIRCE!
I COULD TURN YOU INTO TOADS AND SQUASH YOU ON THE HIGHWAY, BUT I'M FEELING MERCIFUL TODAY!
SO I'LL JUST FREEZE YOU FOR A FEW HOURS AND LET YOU REFLECT ON TALKING BACK TO YOUR BETTERS!
ZAP!
GULP!
HMM! I'VE HEARD THAT A WITCH'S REAL POWER COMES FROM HER BROOMSTICK!
GASP! ONE OF THEM ESCAPED THE EFFECTS OF MY SPELL!
YEAH! AND I'VE GOT A TRICK OR TWO OF MY OWN!

LIKE THIS DISAPPEARING BROOM TRICK FOR EXAMPLE! HAR!
SCREECH!
BUZZ!
GROAN! ENCHANTED BROOMS ARE SO HARD TO COME BY THESE DAYS!
BAH! I'M GOING HOME! IF EVEN THOSE DIMWITS CAN FRUSTRATE ME, I DON'T STAND A CHANCE AGAINST McDUCK!
DON'T WORRY, BROTHERS! I'LL TAKE GOOD CARE OF YOU UNTIL THE SPELL WEARS OFF! I JUST HOPE IT'S SOON!
AND SO...
GOOD! THINGS LOOK NICE AND QUIET AROUND HERE!
I GATHER YOU DIDN'T HAVE ANY TROUBLE, NEPHEW?
JUST WITH BOREDOM, UNCLE SCROOGE! IT SURE HAS BEEN QUIET AROUND HERE!
King Arthur
IT FACT, I WAS WISHING FOR A LITTLE EXCITEMENT! WHY COULDN'T I HAVE BEEN A BRAVE KNIGHT REPELLING AN ATTACK ON YOUR TREASURE BY LOOTERS AND EVIL MAGICIANS?
DREAM ON, DONALD! LUCKILY FOR ME, THINGS LIKE THAT DON'T HAPPEN ANY MORE!
The End

THE WET BET
WALT DISNEY
GOING PLACES with Arizona Dipp
IT 2311-02
HAH! SEE? I TOLD YOU SO!
OKAY, OKAY! YOU WIN TH' BET! YOU WERE RIGHT, I WAS WRONG!
-SIGH!- SHE DOES EXIST!
NOW WILL YA STOP RUBBING IT IN MY FACE?
LOCH NESS
THE END

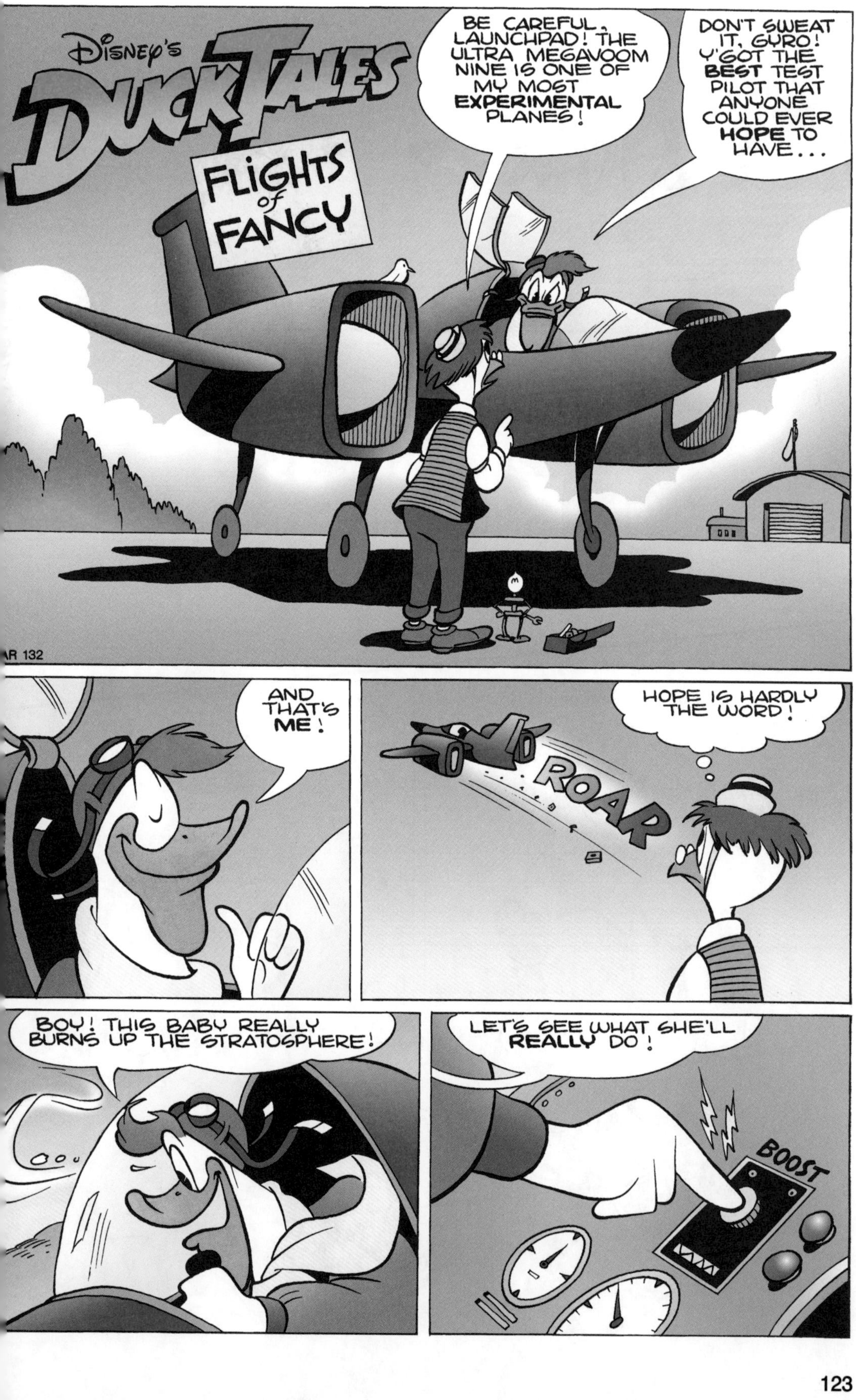

DISNEY'S DUCKTALES
FLIGHTS of FANCY
BE CAREFUL, LAUNCHPAD! THE ULTRA MEGAVOOM NINE IS ONE OF MY MOST EXPERIMENTAL PLANES!
DON'T SWEAT IT, GYRO! Y'GOT THE BEST TEST PILOT THAT ANYONE COULD EVER HOPE TO HAVE...
AR 132
AND THAT'S ME!
HOPE IS HARDLY THE WORD!
ROAR
BOY! THIS BABY REALLY BURNS UP THE STRATOSPHERE!
LET'S SEE WHAT SHE'LL REALLY DO!
BOOST

VROOM
MACH ONE!
PHASE ONE LOOKS GOOD, LAUNCHPAD! GO AHEAD TO PHASE TWO!
ROGER!
PHASE TWO INITIATED!
SUPER BOOST
MACH TWO, AND PRETTY AS YOU PLEASE!
ZOOW
OKAY, LAUNCHPAD! COME ON DOWN! WE DON'T HAVE TO DO EVERYTHING THE FIRST TIME UP!
EVERYTHING? HMM!
GO FOR IT
LAUNCHPAD, YOU RASCAL YOU! YOU'RE GONNA DO IT, AIN'TCHA?
INITIATING PHASE THREE, GYRO!
LAUNCHPAD! WAIT!
GO FOR IT

YEE HAH! RIDE 'EM COWBOY!
VA-VOOM
WOW! SUB-ORBITAL!
AND NOW, FOR THE COUP DE GRACE — I'LL KNOCK GYRO'S SOCKS OFF WITH A CLASS 'A' POWER DIVE!
BUT ALAS!
YIPES!
SPUT
FONK
CLANK
WHAT DO I DO NOW, GYRO? THIS THING HAS BLOWN A FUSE, OR SOMETHING!
I DON'T KNOW, LAUNCHPAD! BUT DO SOMETHING! — ANYTHING!
RIGHT! ANYTHING!
ZINK
BAM
FOOP
PUNCH
BUT NOT THIS!

OOPS!
SPRANG
MERE MINUTES LATER
WELL, GYRO, WHAT'S NEXT?
NOTHING, YOU LUNKHEAD! YOU PUSHED TOO HARD!
BUT I GOTTA PUSH, GYRO! THAT'S WHAT BEING A TEST PILOT IS ALL ABOUT!
HMF!
COME ON, OL' BUDDY! GIMME ANOTHER FLIGHT! A GUY LIKE ME HAS TO STAY UP THERE, OR I'M NOTHING!
STAY UP, EH? HMM!
AND SO—
YAHOO! LOOKIT ME GO, GYRO! A QUARTER OF A MILE AN HOUR AND THE SKY'S THE LIMIT!
I SUPPOSE FOR SOME IT'S THE CHALLENGE!

WALT DISNEY'S
UNCLE $CROOGE
in
"His Fortune On The Rocks"
THERE IT IS, BOYS... THE MOUNTAIN I BOUGHT FROM THE SNEE-KAH INDIANS, ALONG WITH SOME OIL RIGHTS!
AR 128
SNEE-KAH PEAK! I DIDN'T ANT IT, BUT THEY INSISTED ON MAKING IT PART OF THE DEAL!
THEY SOUND PRETTY SHREWD!
THEY *ARE!* THEY'RE USING MY MONEY TO BUILD A DELUXE DESERT *RESORT* AND A *HIGHWAY* INTO TOWN FOR THE TOURISTS!
SNEE KAH
Opening Soon! SNEE-KAH WAY
HAT'S A MIGHTY BLEAK PEAK, NCA SCROOGE! DON'T YOU OWN ANY *OTHER* DESERT LAND?
JUST A SINGLE HUNDRED-ACRE TRACT!
BEEP! BEEP!
McD
THAT'S NOT A LOT OF LAND FOR SCROOGE McDUCK! WHERE'S IT LOCATED?
DOWNTOWN PHOENIX!

I'VE NEVER BOUGHT ANYTHING I COULDN'T MAKE A PROFIT ON AND I DON'T INTEND TO LET THIS HUNK OF ROCK SPOIL MY RECORD!
SCREECH!
Z.
THAT'S WHY I BROUGHT YOU BOYS ALONG! YOU'RE TO HELP ME SCOUT THE MOUNTAIN FOR SOMETHING VALUABLE!
HSSSS
SURE! WE'LL CHECK FOR MINERAL AND GEM DEPOSITS!
AAH... WHADDA' YOU MICROBES KNOW ABOUT ROCKS?
WE'RE FIVE-STAR C.R.A.K.E.R.J.A.C.S. IN THE JUNIOR WOODCHUCKS!
CONNOISSEUR ROCK-HOUNDS AND ALL-KNOWING EXPERTS IN RECOGNIZING JEWELS AND ALL CHOICE STONES!
EXCELLENT! I KNEW YOU'D BE HELPFUL!
THAT'S NOTHING! I WAS QUITE THE ROCK EXPERT IN MY DAY!
THE LITTLE BONEHEADS NAMED ME CHAMPION ROCKHOUND AND ADEPT COLLECTOR OF KEEN PEBBLES AND OTHER TREASURES!
YOU WERE A C.R.A.C.K.P.O.T.?
I DON'T LIKE TO BRAG, BUT AHEM...
I STARTED MY FORTUNE AS A PROSPECTOR BUT THESE OLD BONES NEED A LITTLE HELP TO CLIMB MOUNTAINS NOWADAYS!

HE CLIMBING GEAR
IS IN MY JEEP!
HOLD ON! I'M NOT CLIMBING THAT PEAK FOR YOUR USUAL THIRTY CENTS AN HOUR!
FINE! BUT THE TAXI FARE BACK TO TOWN FOR NON-EMPLOYEES IS STEEPER THAN THOSE SLOPES!
TIK
TIK
McDUCK TAXI CO.
$$$
SIGH!
THIS WILL BE A GREAT ADVENTURE!
MAYBE!... IT DOESN'T LOOK PROMISING!
THE MOUNTAIN IS SO FULL OF CRACKS AND FAULTS THAT IT'LL BE DANGEROUS CLIMBING!
YOU'RE RIGHT! OOK AT ALL THOSE FRACTURES!
AT LEAST WE CAN DRIVE OUR PITONS IN 'EM!
LET'S GET STARTED!
SO WHERE DO I HAMMER THIS SPIKE?
RIGHT THERE, UNCA DONALD! THAT'S YOUR FAULT!
OH, SURE! BLAME EVERYTHING ON ME!

SOME TIME AND CONFUSION LATER...
GENERAL DEWEY, NAME THREE TYPES OF ROCK!
IGNEOUS! METAMORPHIC! SEDIMENTARY! GENERAL LOUIE, NAME THE METAMORPHIC ROCKS!
SLATE, QUARTZ GNEISS, MARBLE...
QUIET UP THERE! UNCLE SCROOGE IS TRYING TO CONCENTRATE!
OOT-SKREET
TSK! THIS IS DISCOURAGING! NO SILVER! NO COPPER! NO IRON! JUST ROCK!
LET'S COMB THIS LEDGE!
WOW! I FOUND AN EMERALD!
PHOOEY! IT'S ONLY THE AMAZONITE VARIETY OF ORTHOCLASE, TOO FLAWED TO BE WORTH ANYTHING!
THERE'S A LOT OF CHERT HERE, THOUGH
THAT'S WHAT THE INDIANS USED TO MAKE ARROWHEADS!
HEY! THAT COULD MEAN BIG BUCKS FROM GREENHORN TOURISTS!
TOSS SOME SAMPLES ON MY BACKPACK AND I'LL CHECK TO SEE IF WE HAVE ANY INDIAN RELICS!

BAH! THESE ARE JUST WORTHLESS ROCKS!
CAN I HAVE A SAMPLE OF WHATEVER YOU'VE FOUND?
I'M SURE UNCA SCROOGE WOULD GIVE YOU THE CHERT OFF HIS PACK!
HA! NOT THE UNCLE SCROOGE I KNOW!
SO, I MEAN...
SKIP IT! LET'S CHECK OUT THIS CAVE!
EUREKA! IT'S STUDDED WITH DIAMONDS! JUST LOOK AT 'EM SPARKLE!
HERE'S THE FLASH-LIGHT!
ULP!!
YOW!!
WHAT'S THAT?
LOOKS LIKE SMOKE SIGNALS FROM THAT RICH DUCK ON HIS MOUNTAIN! CAN YOU READ IT?
YOU KIDDING? I MAJORED IN CIVIL ENGINEERING! BESIDES, IF McDUCK IS INSPECTING THAT WORTHLESS MOUNTAIN, I'M SURE HE'S NOT SAYING ANYTHING POLITE!

LATER...
SO IT'S AGREED! WE DON'T GO IN CAVES!
HEY... WHAT'S THAT?
THERE'S SOMETHING RED ON THAT OUTCROPPING!
I'M GOING TO CHECK IT OUT!
BE CAREFUL, UNCA SCROOGE!
DON'T WORRY! WE'RE TIED TOGETHER!
LOOKS LIKE A GARNET! OR A RUBY!!! OR...
DONALD! WHERE DID YOU THROW THAT BUBBLE GUM YOU WERE CHEWING?
OOPS... SORRY!
HURRY UP, UNCA SCROOGE! I DON'T LIKE THE LOOKS OF THE HAIRLINE CRACK IN THIS ROCK!
HAIRLINE NOTHING! LOOKS LIKE ABOUT AN EIGHTH OF AN INCH!
OR MAYBE HALF AN INCH! UH-OH!
UNCA SCROOGE!

H, MY
TARS!
CRAK!
I DID MENTION THERE WAS NO HAZARD PAY, DIDN'T I?
ERG!
TWANG!
TRY TO SWING OVER AND GRAB THE CLIFF FACE, UNCA SCROOGE!
NOW WHAT?
CRASH!
HERE GOES... GRUNT!

PERFECT! I'LL GRAB THE LEDGE AND...
OF ALL THE DAD-BLAMED PLACES TO PUT A GOAT!
?!
WAK!!
STAND STILL, YOU HORNED FLEABAG!
YEEK!
KLONK!
DON'T LET GO, UNCA SCROOGE!
OUCH! IT MIGHT BE LESS PAINFUL IF WE FALL!
BONK!
?
HUEY! GRAB THAT ROCK!
GOT IT!!!

OOG!
REAK!
ZOW!
THWIP!
WOW! LOOK AT THAT GOAT GO! JUST LIKE CRACKING THE WHIP!
WHERE'S UNCA SCROOGE?
ARE YOU OKAY, UNCA SCROOGE?
WELL, PERHAPS IF YOU LOOSENED THIS ROPE JUST A TRIFLE...
WHEW!
SAY, LOOK WHAT THE CHAMPEEN ROCKHOUND FOUND IN THIS CRAG...
...A HUGE OPAL!
DON'T HURT HER, UNCA DONALD! SHE'S AN ENDANGERED SPECIES!
GLEEP!
WHAT DO YOU CALL ME?

OH, NO, MISSUS EAGLE! NOT IN THERE!
LOB!
YOW!
FOONT!
LOOK! MORE SMOKE SIGNALS!
IT'S THAT BIGSHOT DUCK AGAIN, TRYING TO BE THE CENTER OF ATTENTION! IGNORE HIM!
FINALLY, MANY HOURS LATER...
DRAT AND DOUBLE DRAT! WE'RE AT THE SUMMIT AND WE HAVEN'T FOUND SO MUCH AS A RHINESTONE OFF A COW-BOY'S SHIRT!
LET'S START BACK DOWN AND CHECK EVEN CLOSER!
WHAT'S THIS COLORFUL ROCK?
THAT'S GNEISS!
I THINK IT'S NICE, TOO, BUT WHAT IS IT?
NO, I MEAN THAT'S A GNEISS ROCK! THE ROCK IS GNEISS! IT'S JUST PLAIN GNEISS!
JEEPERS! IF YOU'RE THAT CRAZY ABOUT IT, HERE... IT'S YOURS!
I SEE SOMETHING!

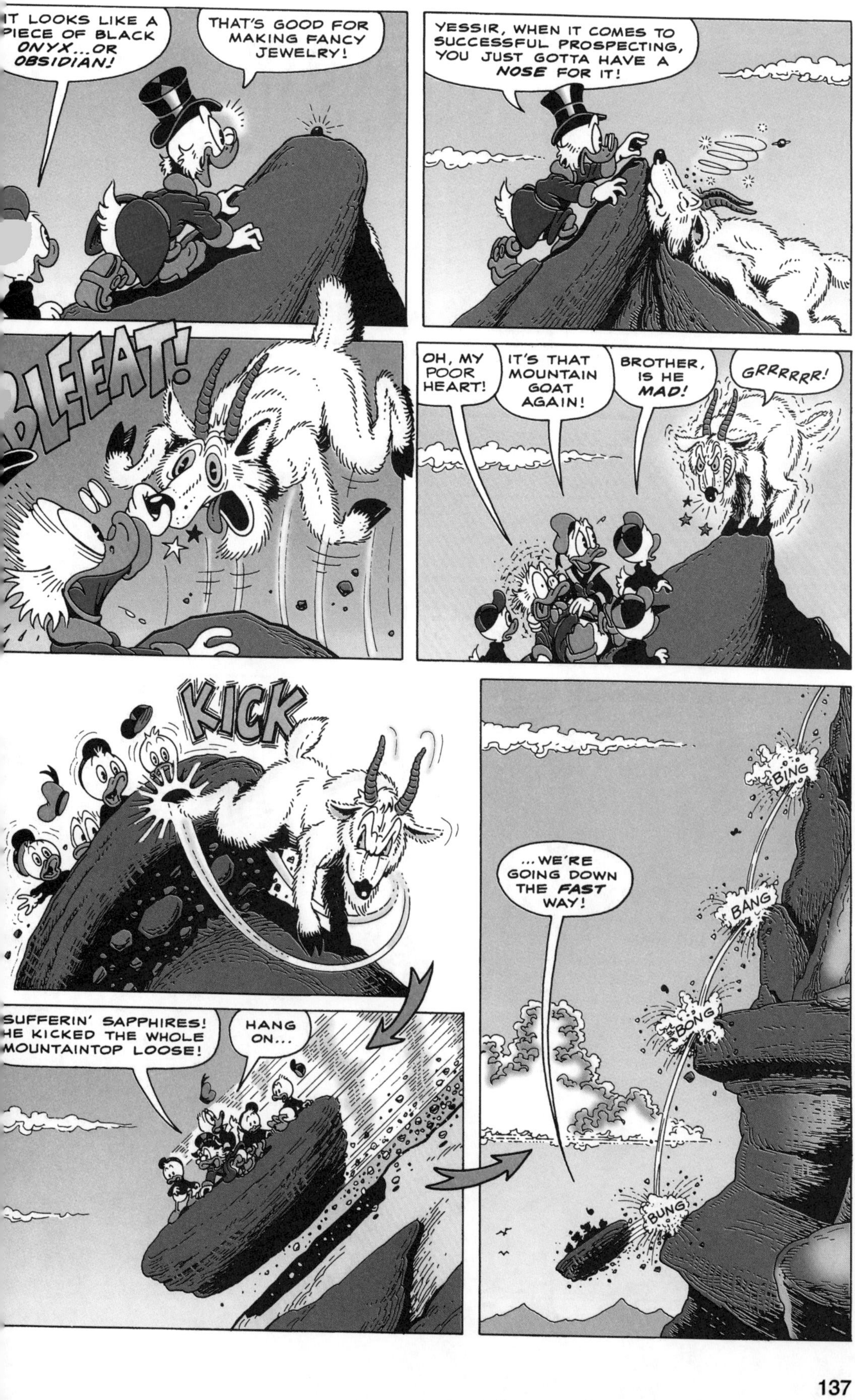

IT LOOKS LIKE A PIECE OF BLACK ONYX...OR OBSIDIAN!
THAT'S GOOD FOR MAKING FANCY JEWELRY!
YESSIR, WHEN IT COMES TO SUCCESSFUL PROSPECTING, YOU JUST GOTTA HAVE A NOSE FOR IT!
BLEEAT!
OH, MY POOR HEART!
IT'S THAT MOUNTAIN GOAT AGAIN!
BROTHER, IS HE MAD!
GRRRRRR!
KICK
SUFFERIN' SAPPHIRES! HE KICKED THE WHOLE MOUNTAINTOP LOOSE!
HANG ON...
...WE'RE GOING DOWN THE FAST WAY!
BING
BANG
BONG
BUNG

ZOW!
CRASH!
BOOMF!
GROAN! MY BACK!
WHAT ARE YOU SMILING ABOUT?
IMAGINE WHAT THAT DESCENT SAVED ME IN HOURLY WAGES!
TILT
BUT SOB! I OWN A WHOLE MOUNTAIN OF NOTHING BUT WORTHLESS, FRACTURED ROCK!
HEY, THERE!
SNEE-KAH HIGHWAY CONSTRUCTION
HOW MUCH IS YOUR GRAVEL? IT WILL SAVE US THE 150-MILE TRIP INTO TOWN!
AND SO...
YOU SEE, KIDS, I ALWAYS TURN A PROFIT!
IT'S A MIGHTY SMALL PROFIT!
McDUCK'S GRAVEL CO. $50 PER LOAD NO OVERHEAD! JUST SKY!
SNEE-KAH HIGHWAY CONSTRUCTION
BUT THAT'S A MIGHTY BIG MOUNTAIN! BESIDES, I'M HOLDING DOWN THE OVERHEAD!
THE GRAVEL BIN'S GETTING LOW! TELL DONALD TO START UP THE ROCK-CRUSHER!
UNCA DONALD...
I HEARD HIM! I HEARD HIM!
ROCK CRUSHER

Walt Disney's
Donald Duck
in
The Leaning Tower of Meatloaf
INNER TIME T THE DUCK OUSE!
HUNGRY, BOYS?
I'M SO STARVED I COULD EAT A HOUSE!
I COULD EAT TWO HOUSES!
I COULD EAT AN ENTIRE APARTMENT BUILDING AND STILL HAVE ROOM FOR DESSERT!
93233
THEN GET READY FOR SOME GOOOOOD GRUB! MY FAMOUS MOUTH-WATERIN', RIB-STICKIN', BELLY-BUSTIN'–
MEATLOAF?! YUCK!
B-BUT YOU KIDS ADORE MY MEATLOAF! WHAT'S WITH THE PICKY PALATES?
WE'RE EARNING OUR NEW JUNIOR WOODCHUCK BADGES IN GOURMET CUISINE!
WE NOW PREFER TO TANTALIZE OUR TASTEBUDS...
...NOT ANNIHILATE THEM!
SHALL WE REPAIR TO CHEZ DUCKBURG FOR SOME EDIBLE EATABLES, GENTS?
INDUBITABLY!

THE NEXT MORNING!
YOU'RE A COOK, JOE—WHADDAYA KNOW ABOUT GOURMET GRUB?
ONLY THIS, DONALD: IT'S ALL IN THE NAME!
Joe's Java Joint
Fromage-Burger
Haute Dog
Pommes Frites
CREPES SUZETTE ARE JUST FANCY FLAPJACKS! AND ESCARGOT? GARDEN SLUGS!
JOE! SIX ORDER OF POMMES FRITES, THREE HAUTE DOGS, FOUR FROMAGE-BURGERS, AND A MUGGA JAVA!
SEE WHAT I MEAN?
SHUCKS, I COULD SELL DIRTY DISHWATER IF I CALLED IT SOMETHIN' SWANKY!
THANKS, JOE! SOUNDS MAGNIFIQUE TO THIS MAN—I MEAN, THIS MONSIEUR!
THAT EVENING!
I MUST ADMIT, UNCA DONALD, TONIGHT'S MENU SOUNDS DIVINE!
AND HOW! WHAT'S "PATÉ LE BOEUF"?
MY LATEST SPECIALTY! A TASTEBUD-TEMPTING PALATE-PLEASING, GOURMET-GRATIFYING...
...MEATLOAF? YUCK!
THE ARROGANCE! -SNORT!-
COME ALONG, CHAPS! LET US SEEK A MORE REWARDING REPAST!
CRASH!

NEXT DAY!
MAYBE THE BOYS WOULD LIKE THIS MEATLOAF, DONALD! THE PILGRIMS BROUGHT THE RECIPE OVER ON THE MAYFLOWER!
WELL, THERE'S NO ARGUING WITH HISTORY! I'LL GIVE IT A SHOT!
AND SO...
BOYS, TONIGHT YOU WILL EXPERIENCE THE FOOD OF THE PAST...
OH, GREAT! LEFTOVERS AGAIN!
TA-DAAA! MEATLOAF PILGRIM-STYLE!
TSK TSK, NCA DONALD! HE PILGRIMS NEVER ATE MEATLOAF!
HOW DO YOU KNOW? WERE YOU THERE?
NO, AND THANK GOODNESS FOR SMALL FAVORS! THAT THING LOOKS AS SOLID AS PLYMOUTH ROCK!
-HMPH!- MERELY A TOUCH OVERDONE, THAT'S ALL! -OOF!-
REST ASSURED THAT UNDER THIS- UH, STURDY CRUST IS A MEATLOAF THAT'LL GO DOWN IN THE RECORD BOOKS! -UNK!-
WHACK!
RECORD BOOKS, INDEED! WHAT DO WE LOOK UNDER..."M" FOR MYSTERY MEAT?
TRY "C" – FOR CATASTROPHE!

NEVER ONE TO ADMIT DEFEAT, DONALD TRIES ANOTHER STRATEGY!
MONSIEUR DUCK! FOR THE LAST TIME, MEATLOAF IS NOT IN OUR CURRICULUM!
DUCKBURG ACADEMY OF HAUGHTY CUISINE
CAN'T YOU GIMME JUST ONE HOITY-TOITY TIP? PLEEEEASE??
OH, VERY WELL. ALWAYS REMEMBER...
...THE NOSE KNOWS! FINE FOOD IS 99.9% AROMA!
...TEN POUNDS OF ONIONS, SIXTEEN HEADS OF GARLIC, AND ONE WHEEL OF LIMBURGER CHEESE! WAIT TILL THOSE SUPERSNOOTS TASTE THIS MEATLOAF!
HECK, THEY WON'T EVEN HAVE TO TASTE IT! JUST THE SMELL WILL BE PLENTY!
A FEW HOURS LATER!
PHEW! WHAT A HORRIBLE STENCH!
A HAZARDOUS TOXIC LEAK, NO DOUBT! WE'D BETTER CALL THE AUTHORITIES...
...AND TELL 'EM TO COME TO OUR HOUSE! YIKES!
DONALD DUCK
AND SO...
SOLDIERS, I SMELL VICTORY! CHAAARGE!!!

-AHH!- WHAT A WONDERFUL AROMA! DID ANY ROSE EVER SMELL AS SWEE-
EEEEEK!!
SMASH!
OKAY, PAL! DROP THE STINK BOMB AND NOBODY GETS HURT!
STINK BOMB?? IT'S A MEATLOAF, YOU MORON!
AND I'LL NEVER GIVE IT UP! DO YOU HEAR ME? NEVER!!!!
SIZZLE!
THEN FEAST ON THIS FRAGRANCE, FIEND: "EAU DE ROSES"!
DON'T SHOOT! I'M ALLERGIC TO-
SQUIRT!
SQUIRT!
WAAH-CHOOOOO!!
ANOTHER MEATLOAF, UNCA DONALD? TSK!
WILL YOU NEVER LEARN?
SUCH JUVENILE BEHAVIOR! IT TRULY TRIES THE PATIENCE!
UNQUESTIONABLY!

THE MORNING AFTER!
LOOK, FELLOW EPICURES! DUCKBURG ART INSTITUTE HAS A NEW EXHIBIT CALLED "THE ART OF FOOD"!
FOOD AND ART? BE STILL, MY HEART!
HURRY, MEN! AN EVENT LIKE THIS COMES BUT ONCE IN A LIFETIME!
OH, YEAH? JUST YOU WAIT!
THAT EVENING!
UNCA DONALD! WHAT'S GOING ON?
ONLY THE ARTISTIC EVENT OF THE SEASON, BOYS... I'M ABOUT TO UNVEIL MY LATEST WORK! COME IN AND SEE FOR YOURSELVES!
WILL IT TAKE LONG? WE'RE KINDA IN A HURRY...
I AM BREVITY ITSELF, LADS. NOW STEP RIGHT UP FOR THE THRILL OF YOUR LIVES!
-AHEM!- FRIENDS, CONNOISSEURS, GOURMANDS! WHAT YOU ARE ABOUT TO WITNESS HAS NO EQUAL IN THE WORLD OF FOOD OR ART! PREPARE TO BE DAZZLED BY THE MOST SUBLIME, THE MOST MAJESTIC, THE MOST-
UNCA DONALD!!
CAN'T YOU PICK UP THE PACE A BIT? WE REALLY HAVE TO LEAVE SOON!
OKAY, OKAY! WITHOUT FURTHER ADO, MAY I PROUDLY PRESENT...

...THE LEANING TOWER OF MEATLOAF!
GASP!!!
UH... NICE JOB, UNCA DONALD, BUT WE GOTTA GO TO BURGERAMA NOW!
BURGERAMA??! THAT TWO-BIT HASH HOUSE? BUT I THOUGHT YOU STUCK-UPPERS ONLY ATE FINICKY FOOD!
NOT ANYMORE—NOW WE'RE WORKING ON JUNIOR WOODCHUCK URBAN SURVIVAL BADGES!
AND WE HAFTA EAT FAST FOOD FOR FIVE DAYS STRAIGHT. IT'S A REQUIREMENT!
BUT BOYS! DON'T YOU WANNA EVEN TASTE MY TOWER OF MEATLOAF?
SORRY, UNCA DONALD! OUR GARBAGE-BURGERS AWAIT!
BON APPETIT!
I SAY! DO YOU KNOW WHAT THAT MEANS, GOURMANDS?
CHOW TIME FOR US!!
HEY! STOP, YOU VULTURES! STOP!!

I'M SAVING THAT FOR MY NEPHEWS, YOU MUNCHING MUSHMOUTHS!
BUT WE'VE ALWAYS WANTED TO EAT GREAT ART!
SHOW SOME CLASS, MADAM! WOULD YOU CHOMP ON THE SISTINE CHAPEL?
IF IT HAD KETCHUP ON IT, YOU BET!
TIM-BERRRR!
HOLY HAMBURGER! LOOK OUT!!
NEXT DAY!
DUCKBURG GAZETTE
THREE INJURED IN MEATLOAF MELEE!
WE'VE BEEN HIDING HERE SINCE LAST NIGHT! THINK IT'S SAFE TO GO HOME YET?
NO WAY! UNCA DONALD'S STILL MADDER THAN A FLY IN A FONDUE POT!
BUT I'M STARVING
I'M SO HUNGRY I COULD EAT A HOUSE!
I COULD EAT TWO HOUSES!
MAN! I COULD EVEN EAT...MEATLOAF!

UNCLE $CROOGE
Much Ado About Telepathy
H9122
UP AND AT 'EM, LAZY BONES! TIME FOR AN ADVENTURE!
IZZAT SO!
I NEED YOU BOYS IN THE JUNGLE AT SIXTY CENTS AN HOUR!
WHY DIDN'T YOU TELL ME?
COUNT US IN!
WHIT!
SIXTY! THAT'S BIG MONEY FOR YOU!
MOOLAH IS NO OBJECT! I'M AFTER A RARE ANIMAL TODAY!
WHAT KIND? A MINOTAUR?
A FLYING PIG?
A PUFFTAILED WOODSEER, BOYS! I'M STOCKING UP MY ZOO AGAIN!
IS THAT HIM? WHAT A
SOURPUSS!
GLOOMY OR NOT, HE'S OUR MAN!
ECUADOR!
TAXI, MISTER?
I'M LOOKING FOR WOODSEER COUNTRY!
013
YOU WANT THE RAINFOREST, BUDDY! BUT YOU'RE MAKING A MISTAKE!
013

MISTAKE? BAH! WOODSEERS MAY BE RARE, BUT THAT DOESN'T MEAN WE WON'T FIND ONE!
I DON'T THINK THAT'S WHAT OUR DRIVER WAS WORRIED ABOUT!
SURE! HE THOUGHT WE WERE GREENHORNS! WE'LL SHOW HIM!
VOILA!
SUCCESS ALREADY!
SKRITCH SKRITCH
HE'S ON THE LAM! AFTER HIM!
COME BACK HERE, DROOPY-EYES! I NEED YOU!
IS ZOO ATTENDANCE THAT BAD?
PUFF! I'M ALL IN!
US, TOO!
LET THE WOODSEER VAMOOSE! THERE'S MORE WHERE HE CAME FROM!
THIS IS JUST LIKE THE TIME I WAS HUNTING BALM IN GILEAD! IT WAS IN 1919...
GASP!
YOU WERE SAYING ABOUT GILEAD?
I WAS THINKING ABOUT GILEAD! A VOICE OVER THERE JUST SAID WHA I WAS THINKING!

JUMPIN' JACKSNIPES!
IT'S THE WOODSEER! HE'S BACK FOR SOME REASON!
HE'S CUTE... IN A SLEEPY KINDA WAY!
MAN, MAN! WAIT TILL DAISY HEARS ABOUT THIS!
HE... HE TALKS!
HE REPEATS WHAT WE SAY, LIKE SOME LONGHAIRED PARROT!
I BET ZOOGOERS WOULD PAY EXTRA FOR A LOOK AT HIM!
STOP THE PRESSES!
THIS LAZY VARMINT'S READING OUR MINDS!
HE'S AT IT AGAIN!
HE'S NOT REPEATING WHAT WE SAY! HE'S GOT TELEPATHY! HE'S REPEATING WHAT WE THINK!
NO WONDER HE'S CALLED A SEER!
YOU'D ALMOST THINK ONE OF US WAS A VENTRILO-QUIST, PLAYING SOME COCKEYED CON GAME!
WAK! I WAS THINKING THAT!
US, TOO!
PICKLE-NOSE, YOU AND I WERE MEANT FOR EACH OTHER!
WITH YOU AT MY SIDE, WILL I EVER HAVE POWER! HEH, HEH, HEH!

WITH HIM AT YOUR SIDE?
UNCA SCROOGE WANTS THIS LITTLE GUY FOR SLAVE LABOR!
HE'S GOING IN THE ZOO... RIGHT?
B-BUT OF COURSE, LADS! HE'LL BE FROLICKING WITH HIS ANIMAL PALS!
FROLICKING IN MY MONEY BIN, THAT IS!
THAT'S OUTTA THE QUESTION, UNK!
IT'S NOT FAIR!
SURE IT IS! ⊰SNORT!⊱ I ONLY WANT TO KNOW MY BUSINESS RIVALS' INNERMOST THOUGHTS!
AND IF THAT MEANS CAGING UP THIS FURRY FINK, SO BE IT!
HE'S BUILT FOR THE WILD! NOT FOR THE OFFICE!
CONFOUND MY SOFTHEARTED NEPHEWS!
AND TO THINK I'M PAYING THEM SIXTY CENTS AN HOUR!
OR... ⊰HEH! HEH!⊱ SO THEY BELIEVE!
HUH?!
EGAD!
WHEN THEY ASK ME TO PAY THEM, I'LL DISAVOW ALL KNOWLEDGE OF HOW MUCH I OFFERED!
SO!
AS THE SUN SINKS SLOWLY IN THE WEST!
YOU LOOK AWFUL, McDUCK! WHERE'S THE WOODSEER?
GONE! AND CONSIDER YOURSELF LUCKY! YOU DON'T WANT TO HEAR WHAT I'M THINKING!
013

WALT DISNEY'S
MICKEY MOUSE
IN WITH FRIENDS LIKE THESE...
AH, MICKEY, THERE YOU ARE! I'VE BEEN LOOKING ALL OVER FOR YOU!
OH! Uh... HI, MINNIE!
BOUQUET BOUTIQUE
WANT TO COME OVER FOR DINNER TONIGHT? I HAVE A GREAT NEW RECIPE I'M DYING TO TRY OUT!
UM... Uh... SORRY, MINNIE... I CAN'T! I... ER... PROMISED TO DO SOMETHING ELSE TONIGHT!
WELL -GIGGLE!- AS LONG AS YOU BOUGHT ME FLOWERS, I GUESS I DON'T MIND!
-ULP!-
THE TRUTH IS, MINNIE, THESE FLOWERS ARE FOR... FOR... SOMEONE ELSE!
?
I... I CAN'T EXPLAIN NOW, BUT I... I'LL CALL YOU TOMORROW! BYE!

THAT'S ODD... IT'S NOT LIKE MICKEY TO BE SO SECRETIVE!
I MEAN, WHY SHOULD I CARE IF HE BOUGHT FLOWERS FOR SOMEONE ELSE! THEY'RE PROBABLY FOR HIS COUSIN MADELINE, ANYWAY!
SALE!
SURE, THAT'S IT... MADELINE'S IN TOWN ON A VISIT AND HE'S BUSY TONIGHT ENTERTAINING HER!
SILLY BOY! WHY DIDN'T HE JUST TELL ME? DOES HE THINK I'M STILL JEALOUS OF HER?
SALE!
Hm... A DOZEN LONG-STEMMED RED ROSES IS A BIT TOO ROMANTIC A BOUQUET TO GIVE TO A COUSIN! YOU DON'T SUPPOSE...
R. S'CARPA
NO! GET A GRIP ON YOURSELF, GIRL! I'M SURE THERE'S A VERY INNOCENT REASON FOR THAT BOUQUET!
LIKE... LIKE... LIKE...
BOO-HOO-HOO! MICKEY'S FOUND A NEW GIRLFRIEND!

MINNIE! Oh, DEAR... WHATEVER IS THE MATTER?
NOTHING, DOC! NOTHING EXCEPT... EXCEPT ⇒SNIFF!⇐ MICKEY'S DUMPED ME!
WATERWORKS
AND ALL THIS TIME I THOUGHT MY ONLY COMPETITION WAS YOU AND YOUR CRAZY EXPERIMENTS!
IMPOSSIBLE! MICKEY IS DEVOTED TO YOU! THAT'S A PROVABLE SCIENTIFIC FACT!
THE FACTS ARE HE'S SEEING ANOTHER WOMAN TONIGHT, AND HE BOUGHT ROSES FOR HER! HOW DOES THAT PROVE HIS DEVOTION?
HAVE YOU SEEN THIS "OTHER WOMAN"?
WELL, NO, BUT...
THERE YOU GO! IN SCIENCE, WHATEVER HAS NOT BEEN OBSERVED IS ONLY CONJECTURE!
I SUSPECT THE SAME HOLDS TRUE FOR AFFAIRS OF THE HEART!
WELL... MICKEY DID SAY HE'LL CALL ME TOMORROW AND EXPLAIN!
I'LL GIVE HIM THE BENEFIT OF THE DOUBT UNTIL THEN! THANKS, DOC!
POOR, POOR MINNIE!

INVENTOR'S SUPPLY
YOUR ONE-STOP CRACKPOT SHOP
HEY, DOC! DON'T JUST STAND THERE— GIVE ME A HAND! AFTER ALL, THIS IS YOUR STUFF!
BOLTS 50% OFF
ASK ABOUT OUR NUTS
THAT'S THE TROUBLE WITH WORKING FOR A SCIENTIST! YOU'RE ALWAYS OFF IN DREAM-LAND PLANNING YOUR NEXT KOOKY EXPERIMENT!
NO, NO... IT'S NOT THAT...
I WAS JUST THINKING HOW UPSET MINNIE WOULD BE IF SHE KNEW THAT JUST THIS MORNING, I HELPED MICKEY BETRAY HER!
BANG! BONG! CLONG!
WAKE UP, DOC! I NEED YOU TO WHIP UP A FORMULA FOR ME!
BONG!
CLONG!
I REMEMBER YOU TELLING ME ABOUT PHEROMONES— NATURAL CHEMICALS SOME ANIMALS GIVE OFF TO ATTRACT A MATE!
I WANT YOU TO MAKE A COLOGNE THAT WILL HAVE THAT SAME EFFECT ON A WOMAN! MAKE WHOEVER WEARS IT IRRESISTIBLE TO HER!
AND I NEED IT FOR TONIGHT, DOC! CAN YOU DO IT?
Hm... LET'S SEE... IF I MIX THREE PARTS EXTRACT OF RHODODENDRON WITH ONE PART DISTILLED SWEAT...

HA-HA-HA! I'LL SAY MINNIE WILL BE UPSET! MICKEY'S GONNA SHOW UP SMELLING LIKE A LOCKER ROOM!
NO, NO... YOU DON'T GET IT! MICKEY'S NOT SEEING MINNIE TONIGHT!
Huh? BUT YOU SAID HE NEEDED THE COLOGNE TONIGHT!
EXACTLY! IT'S POSSIBLE MICKEY IS SEEING ANOTHER WOMAN!
HORSEFEATHERS! MICKEY AND MINNIE GO TOGETHER LIKE... LIKE MEAT AND POTATOES!
YA CAN'T HAVE ONE WITHOUT THE OTHER!
CLANG!
WHY, MICKEY'S JUST PLANNING A SURPRISE FOR MINNIE! LISTEN, I SAW HIM A COUPLE OF HOURS AGO...
MOUSETON OPERA HOUSE
PACKARATTI
LAST NIGHT!
YIPPEE! I GOT THE BEST SEATS IN THE HOUSE!
HAW! SURE YOU DON'T WANT THE BACK ROW SO NO ONE WILL HEAR YOU SNORE?
HORACE! ⇒GULP!⇐ PLEASE DON'T TELL ANYONE ABOUT THESE TICKETS, OKAY?
GOTCHA, PAL! PLANNING A SURPRISE FOR THE LITTLE LADY, Huh?
Um... ER... WELL...
MAYBE I OUGHTA DO LIKEWISE! MIGHT GET ME OUT OF THE DOGHOUSE WITH CLARABELLE...

BUT HORACE! MINNIE LOATHES PACKARATTI! WHICH CONVINCES ME MICKEY IS TAKING SOMEONE ELSE!
WHA... WHAT?!
WHY, THAT DIRTY RAT! HE'S TWO-TIMING A SWELL GAL LIKE MINNIE!
HANG ON, DOC! WE GOTTA DO SOMETHING ABOUT IT!
2391
SQUEAL!
SCREECH!
BUT FIRST, WE NEED TO CONSULT AN EXPERT!
CLARABELLE COW
HORACE HORSECOLLAR! I THOUGHT I TOLD YOU NOT TO COME AROUND FOR AT LEAST A WEEK!
AW, SNOOKUMS...
DON'T YOU "SNOOKUMS" ME! I STILL HAVEN'T FORGIVEN YOU FOR THAT POEM COMPARING MY SKIN TO LEATHER!
SLAM!
BUT SNOOKUMS, I... I HAVE JUICY GOSSIP!
WELL, WHY DIDN'T YOU SAY SO IN THE FIRST PLACE! COME ON IN!

SPILL IT! WHO DID WHAT TO WHOM AND WHY?
Oh, IT'S TERRIBLE... TERRIBLE...
HEY! WHAT'S HE DOING HERE?
I INVITED HIM OVER FOR TEA! NOT THAT IT'S ANY OF YOUR BUSINESS!
YEAH, WELL MAYBE YOU'LL THINK TWICE ABOUT TWO-TIMING ME WHEN YOU HEAR WHY WE'RE HERE!
THE SORDID STORY IS QUICKLY TOLD—
THAT WORM! THAT LOUT! THAT BIG-EARED CASANOVA!
MY SENTIMENTS EXACTLY! THE QUESTION IS, WHAT CAN WE DO ABOUT IT?
WE CAN'T TELL MINNIE, THAT'S FOR SURE! THE POOR LITTLE THING WOULD BE HEART-BROKEN!
BUT... BUT MICKEY WOULD NEVER HURT MINNIE!
OMIGOSH! THERE MUST BE A MICKEY MOUSE IMPOSTOR IN TOWN!
RIDICULOUS! MICKEY'S A MAN, AND ALL MEN ARE BEASTS!
BUT... BUT...
STILL, YOU'VE GIVEN ME AN IDEA OF HOW WE CAN TEACH MICKEY A LESSON HE WON'T SOON FORGET!

THAT NIGHT AT THE OPERA—
WHERE IS HE?
I HOPE WE'RE NOT TOO LATE!
NO, THERE HE COMES NOW! BUT HE'S ALONE!
NOT FOR LONG! JUST LOOK AT THAT... THAT PERSON WAVING TO HIM!
WOW!
MICKEY! DEAR HEART, I'VE DECIDED TO TAKE YOU BACK! A LOVE LIKE OURS DESERVES A SECOND CHANCE!
C-C-CLARABELLE?
I HAD TO BREAK UP WITH HIM BECAUSE MY GREAT BEAUTY ALWAYS LEFT HIM SPEECHLESS!
I... I SEE...
MR. MOUSE! YOU SHOULDN'T BE OUT IN PUBLIC! THAT DISEASE YOU HAVE IS HIGHLY CONTAGIOUS!
HE WON'T BE IN PUBLIC LONG, DOCTOR! I'M ARRESTING HIM ON 127 COUNTS OF BIGAMY!

ALL RIGHT, IMPOSTOR! LET'S SEE WHAT YOU LOOK LIKE UNDER THAT DISGUISE!
OW!
YANK!
GAWRSH! THEY'RE REAL!
WILL SOME-ONE PLEASE TELL ME WHAT'S GOING ON!?!
WE'RE HERE, YOU TWO-BIT LOTHARIO, TO BREAK UP YOUR DATE WITH THAT FLOOZY! SHAME ON YOU!
WHICH FLOOZY?!
Uh... CLARABELLE? IT APPEARS THE... Um... "FLOOZY" IS WITH SOMEONE ELSE!
COME, DEAR! LET'S GET AWAY FROM THOSE LUNATICS!
THEN WHO ARE YOU DATING TONIGHT?!
OMIGOSH! THEY'LL BE HERE ANY MINUTE!
QUICK! YOU'VE GOT TO JUST TRUST ME AND HIDE!
CHIEF O'HARA?!?
WITH A GIRL?!?

I MUST SAY THIS DATE HAS SURPRISED ME, SEAMUS! I NEVER SUSPECTED YOU WERE SUCH A ROMANTIC!
WELL, I HAD A LITTLE HELP...
AND YOUR COLOGNE IS SO MANLY!
YOU... YOU FIXED UP CHIEF O'HARA WITH A DATE?
NO, THE CHIEF FIXED HIMSELF UP! ASKED OUT A VERY NICE WOMAN IN THE PROBATION OFFICE!
BUT THEN HE GOT TO WORRYING ABOUT IMPRESSING HER, SO HE BEGGED ME TO ARRANGE IT ALL!
AND BE ON HAND IN CASE IT WENT WRONG!
BUT FIRST HE SWORE ME TO SECRECY! I HAD TO PROMISE NOT TO TELL ANYONE!
THAT SHOULDN'T HAVE BEEN A PROB-LEM...!!!
SO THAT'S WHY YOU COULDN'T SEE MINNIE TONIGHT?
YOU GOT IT, DOC! I HATED TO KEEP A SECRET FROM HER...
"...BUT I HAVE A FEELING SHE'LL FOR-GIVE ME!"
To Minnie from Mickey
The End